WITHDRAWN

COMMON
AND
COURTLY
LANGUAGE

COMMON

A N D

COURTLY

LANGUAGE

The Stylistics of Social Class in
18th-Century English Literature

Carey McIntosh

upp

UNIVERSITY OF PENNSYLVANIA PRESS
PHILADELPHIA

The excerpt from *Pygmalion* by George Bernard Shaw
is reprinted by permission of the Society of Authors
on behalf of the estate of George Bernard Shaw.

The excerpt from *Out of My League* by George A. Plimpton,
copyright © 1963, 1981 by George A. Plimpton,
is reprinted by permission of Viking Penguin Inc.

Library of Congress Cataloging-in-Publication Data

McIntosh, Carey.
    Common and courtly language.

    Bibliography: p.
    Includes index.
    1. English literature—18th century—History and
criticism.   2. Speech in literature.   3. Social
classes in literature.   4. English language—18th
century—Social aspects.   5. English language—18th
century—Style.   I. Title.
PR448.S72M35   1986   820'.9'352062   85-17857
ISBN 0-8122-7998-0 (alk. paper)

Printed in the United States of America

AFFECTIONATELY DEDICATED TO
MILLICENT CAREY McINTOSH
AND
RUSTIN McINTOSH, M.D.

CONTENTS

ACKNOWLEDGMENTS

Preliminary drafts and condensations of chapters 1 and 3 were presented at a departmental colloquium at the University of California at San Diego in 1976 and at meetings of the North-Eastern Modern Language Association in 1978 and the American Society for Eighteenth-Century Studies in 1984; my thanks to Donald Wesling (UCSD), Edward Jennings (SUNY Albany), and John Richetti (Rutgers) respectively. I owe a substantial debt to Jerry Beasley (Delaware) and Sheridan Baker (Michigan) for astute criticisms of a next-to-last version of the manuscript as a whole. Edward Bloom and Melinda Rabb of Brown University supplied perceptive critiques of a very late revision of chapter 1 on very short notice; I am truly grateful. The instruction and encouragement of Arthur Schwartz and Charles Li (University of California at Santa Barbara) greatly assisted my first attempts to learn about language in general, in 1974–76.

INTRODUCTION

HIGGINS [*becoming excited as the idea grows on him*]. . . . I shall make a duchess of this draggle-tailed guttersnipe.

LIZA [*strongly deprecating this view of her*]. Ah-ah-ah-ow-ow-oo!

HIGGINS [*carried away*]. Yes: in six months—in three if she has a good ear and a quick tongue—I'll take her anywhere and pass her off as anything. We'll start today: now! this moment! Take her away and clean her, Mrs. Pearce. Take all her clothes off and burn them. Ring up Whiteley or somebody for new ones. Wrap her up in brown paper til they come.

LIZA. Youre no gentleman, youre not, to talk of such things. I'm a good girl, I am; and I know what the likes of you are, I do.

(G. B. Shaw)

This book deals with some relations between language and social class in seventeenth- and eighteenth-century British literature. Chapter 1 presents a hypothesis for identifying lower-class language, a theory that for a number of reasons works better after 1750 than before. Chapter 2 describes and documents an upper-class style of writing employed from about 1500 to 1800, a medium for elegance and politeness. Chapter 3 examines some of the ways these ideas apply to specific texts: journals, novels, and letters.

Most people take it for granted that language or linguistic usage had some definite relation with social class in this period. A dairymaid did not talk like a duchess. Polite conversation was something that many people recognized as a valuable activity; the working-class vernacular was known to be quite different. But specific features of upper-class eighteenth-century English and general principles underlying lower-class language of the time have not been studied in any detail.

1

One good reason for the relative scarcity of scholarly research on vulgar, demotic English before 1800 is the scarcity of data: no texts survive. Truly lower-class people of this period did not write at all. On most of the lower rungs of the ladder of social rank, illiteracy was the rule, not the exception. Moreover, we cannot assume that any text purporting to derive from lower-class speakers has not been tidied up and corrected by the transcriber (in the absence of tape recordings or the equivalent).

Even in the twentieth century, written records of lower-class speech are likely to have been at least combed and brushed for neatness, and probably outfitted in a literary costume as well. Here is an excerpt from the unedited transcript of part of a conversation recorded in the 1970s:

> ROGER [to Jim]:   Are you just agreeing because you feel you wanna uh
> JIM: Hm?
> ROGER: You just agreeing?
> JIM: What the hell's *that.*
> AL: It's—Agree ing?
> ROGER: Agreeing.
> JIM: Agree::n.
> ROGER: Yeah.
> AL: With us. Just going along with us.
> JIM: No.
> ROGER: Saying 'yes, yes' hehheh hh hehhh hh hehheh
> JIM: Well, i-i-it's-it's true. Everything he sai(h)d is *true*, so . . .   (Sachs, 708)

Take this, with its hesitations, incompletions, interruptions, overlap, and just plain noise, as a sample of nonliterary lower-class dialogue. Contrast with it an interchange between two unnamed professional baseball players in George Plimpton's *Out of My League* (1961):

> Know something? We've been making book here in the dugout as to when you'd keel over.
> No kidding.

Introduction

Yup. He was sure sweating out there, wasn't he, Billy?
Leaking out of him like it was sawdust.
Sawdust? That was *blood*, man. First time I ever thought
I'd be running in for a mound conference to find out what
was going on was a *funeral service*.
Hey, kid, what'ja think of it, hey? How'd ja like it out
there? Pretty rough, hey?
Really sumpin'.
What'd he say?
Really *sump* in' out there.   (140–41)

In his attempts to represent the language of ordinary folk, Plimpton
is not doing anything different from what most writers of realistic
journalism and fiction do, but that does not mean that those attempts are true to life. Almost all published representations of
ostensibly lower-class English are in some respects literary. The hyperbole of this dialogue smacks of Salinger; its prolix folksiness re-
sembles Mark Twain or a writer in the tradition of rural American
humor. It is mostly full sentences, and wastes no words in repetition, overlap, or incompletenesses. One sentence includes four subordinate clauses. In sum, what purports to be authentic low-class
English, especially in works of literature, often is not the same as a
word-for-word transcription of lower-class English speech.

The same is true for "realistic" representations of lower-class
English in the eighteenth century. Northrop Frye's law that literature imitates other literature, not nature, is confirmed by an examination of chapbooks and popular fiction from 1700 to 1775,
which are widely contaminated with romance. These books, often
cheaply printed in small format, had wide circulation among lower-
middle-class readers looking for entertainment, but incident and
event in such books commonly mimic the habitual actions of heroes
and lovers in chivalric romance. Among Cluer Dicey's numerous
publications is an anonymous *Fortunatus* in which the hero, despite
his humble origins, marries the youngest of the three daughters of
the King of Cyprus—he may claim to have been born in a farm-
house, but princesses are his companions in the narrative, and we
cannot trust him to speak in unadulterated working-class English.
Rogue fiction tends to swagger and strut in abominable polysyllabic
fustian: "handsome she was, and very proportionable; but withal so
impudent, that I was antidoted against lechery" (Head, 68). Popular romances of the time favor overwritten purple prose, not plain

3

homespun: "he found her panting Heart beat measures of consent, her heaving Breast swell to be press'd by his, and every Pulse confess a wish to yield" (1719; in Richetti, 188).

The problem is not that popular writings did not speak to or for the lower classes, but that all such texts felt to some degree the influence of whatever literary or genteel traditions were habitually associated with that genre or medium. Popular narratives "heroicized" their central characters. Moreover, people who wrote and read popular narratives had been exposed as children to notions of correctness, accuracy, and propriety that made a difference in what they would commit to paper or tolerate in their reading.

At the other end of the sociolinguistic spectrum we have texts in abundance but no reliable means to say which of their features are owing to gentle breeding or noble blood, which merely to education and a sensitive ear for language. It can be said of certain eighteenth-century people that they spoke like gentlefolk, or that they dressed like gentlefolk or behaved like gentlefolk; but none of these three traits—language, clothing, manners—is essential to authentic gentility, if gentility is defined in terms of rank in society, not behavior. There were ill-spoken noblemen in the eighteenth century, as there were noblemen with coarse, vulgar manners and (less commonly) noblemen with ill-fitting clothes.[1]

Although straight-from-the-horse's-mouth samples of lower-class English before 1800 do not exist, one can use texts that seem to have been written outside the literary contexts of romance and rogue narrative to develop a hypothetical model of lower-class English, incorporating features that seem generally characteristic of uneducated usage of the time. Chapter 1 develops this model and applies it to *Moll Flanders*. As it happens (not by accident), English that conforms to these rules is the opposite of what refined and correct writers of the time were recommending. Many linguistic features of the most proletarian passages of Moll Flanders's narrative are the same linguistic features that were attacked by middle-class neoclassicists. They may serve as a schema for eighteenth-century lower-class language.

Two problems. (1) Having defined "lower-class English" as X, what do we gain by ferreting out examples of X and calling them lower-class? In other words, isn't this reasoning circular? I acknowledge that it is circular, but not therefore trivial or invalid. Leo Spitzer's "circle of style" is circular in the same way. As historians we do not depend exclusively on any one dimension of eighteenth-

4

century culture to identify something as characteristic of the lower class; we cross-check texts and people with whatever else we know about them to confirm or qualify our original judgment (Laslett, 1976). A relatively simple example: Captain Mirvan's language in Burney's novel *Evelina* (1778) is incorrect and unrefined in the ways our model predicts for lower-class speakers, but his class rank would not be easy to assign if he dressed and behaved like Lord Orville, the superbly genteel hero of the same book.

(2) This model does not do justice to the positive values of lower-class English. It accepts such neoclassical values as correctness, precision, and up-to-dateness, without recognizing the literary and linguistic advantages of informal prose, colloquial and unrefined. I acknowledge this as a deficiency. I have not in this book taken the time or space for appreciation of many such positive qualities. On the other hand, my argument is for the most part descriptive, not judgmental.

The genteel, upper-class locutions identified in chapter 2 may be distinguished from locutions equally refined but merely literary by their clear and near alliance to courtly systems of dependency. What I call "courtly-genteel prose" does not obviously betray its origins or affiliations when it is read as a well-integrated component of uncourtly texts, and so I have included samples of this progeny of the technical language of a courtier's trade from six or eight major contexts, samples published between roughly 1485 and 1795. Taken together, these quotations constitute what seems to me convincing evidence for the association of courtly-genteel prose with upper-class aspirations or ideals.

What *is* the "stylistics of social class"? At present (1985) the term *stylistics* means more or less the same as *style studies*. It has not built up scholarly archives of the sort, either empirical or theoretical, that entitle *linguistics* to be considered a more systematic and (in some of its branches) a more scientific discipline than *language studies*. It does assume, as all style studies do, that manner is not the same as matter, and that we cannot fully understand *what* without understanding *how*. A study in the stylistics of social class looks for meaningful relationships between language or linguistic usage and the social status of speakers or writers within a given text. The terms *language* and *social class*, moreover, may be interpreted in a plain, everyday fashion that makes sense without reference to special problems or a difficult provenance.

Language in this book is the texts written in English before

5

1830 or so. By extrapolating from some of these texts and from our knowledge of constructions specific to spoken English in the twentieth century (Crystal and Davy, 1969), we can generalize about colloquial English before 1800, but our data is exclusively English in its written form. It is also *English* English, not Scots English or Somersetshire English, since southeastern written English had squeezed out northern and western dialects at least two hundred years before. Gaelic, Welsh, and other minority tongues did not at this time qualify for national currency.

The English language under discussion in this book may also be said to subsume a set of grammatical principles or rules that govern both its standard and nonstandard variants. In transformational-generative terms, some of these rules generate well-formed structures or sentences, and others generate the slipshod, ill-formed, or incoherent structures that appear in less elegant texts. Eighteenth-century grammarians devoted much attention to rules intended to decide which constructions were correct, which were out of date, and which belonged more properly to spoken English than to written.

There was plenty of variation in the English of this period. The language was changing, gradually, from Early Modern to Present-day English, from the English of Shakespeare to the English of Burke and Tom Paine; and such changes do not take place uniformly or simultaneously but in many thousands of little ways, particle by particle, inconsistently. However, most nonwritten regional variants of standard English may be safely ignored for purposes of this book, for the same reasons that Gaelic and Welsh may be ignored: they did not find their way into print. We know that Samuel Johnson spoke with a broad Midlands accent ("Who's for *poonch?*" he asked, cheerfully, meaning 'punch', a beverage stronger than tea), and we assume that Boswell's manner of talking reflected his Scots ancestry, but both men wrote the same language, if not in the same style. Their contributions to the sum of all texts written in the eighteenth century were printed and read as if they were the same English as came from the pens of Chesterfield and Defoe.

I understand *social class*, with E. P. Thompson, as a historical phenomenon, not a structure or a category; it is "something which in fact happens" in human relationships (Thompson, 9). For the most part, however, documents and books I deal with either antedate or overlook the struggles between lower-class people and other folk that Thompson expounds in *The Making of the English*

6

Introduction

Working Class (1963). Social class may in fact "happen" quite apart from class consciousness in the modern sense, in a society that is made up of people as clearly differentiated as duchesses and dairymaids were before 1800. The overwhelming majority of texts that demonstrate or assume some relation between language and social class before 1800 were written with the assumption that

> As God hath contrived all the Works of Nature to be useful, and in some manner a Support to each other, by which the whole Frame of the World under his Providence is preserved and kept up; so, among Mankind, our particular Stations are appointed to each of us by God Almighty, wherein we are obliged to act, as far as our Power reacheth, towards the Good of the whole Community. (Swift, *"The Duty of Mutual Subjection"* [1744], 142)

Swift is talking here about social class, among other things—social distinctions among different groups of people, high, middle, and low. He takes these distinctions for granted, even though he could not be counted as one of those who "feel and articulate the identity of their interests as between themselves, and as against other" people (quoting Thompson, 9).

What simplifies my task in this book is the fact that eighteenth-century English differentiates itself in response to social class mainly at the extremes. At the lower end of the spectrum we may infer a resemblance to English spoken by illiterate laborers and fishwives. At the upper end we find verbal links with the court and with courtly ideals.

Upper-class society in seventeenth- and eighteenth-century England is relatively easy to identify. Land ownership, not occupation, was the principal basis for status, political power, and wealth. Upper-class social status may therefore confidently be ascribed to the peerage and the gentry, who were the major landowners, and upper-class linguistic status accrues to any locutions that are unambiguously associated with this elite group. There were never more than 170 peers at any one time before the middle of the eighteenth century, and probably not more than 18,000–23,000 gentry, in a population that was growing from roughly five million to ten million between 1700 and 1800 (Mingay [1963], 3–6).

In the very lowest social classes, among nonliterate working people and unemployed, English was entirely colloquial and en-

7

tirely unregulated. Whatever got the message across was acceptable, including slang, profanity, dialect, thieves' cant, grunts, signs, gestures, jargon, and quotations from the Bible.

Between this tiny upper class and this numerous, uncounted lower class is the domain of what we now think of as English, in its ordinary, mutable state or states. This study will concentrate on two forms of systematic variation from the most commonplace norms of this middle-class English, "barbarous," vulgar locutions at one extreme, and phrases that proclaim an affiliation with the upper class, the landed elite, at the other.

It should be acknowledged from the beginning that relations between language and social class are never merely mechanical, and any general hypothesis we discover will have exceptions. Both variants crop up almost from top to bottom of any sociolinguistic hierarchy one chooses to postulate. That is, we can find examples of lower-class English in countesses and peers; and even Partridge, a good representative of the bottom rung of the middle class, could claim to "write Gentleman" after his name, presumably because he had been a schoolteacher and knew some Latin (see *Tom Jones*, 1:515; bk. 9, ch. 6). The freedom and mobility of English society in the eighteenth century, compared for example to French society of the same period, permitted gifted plebeians to rise to the gentry or beyond and peers to imitate their lower-class cousins in language as well as manners, if they pleased.

Within these limits, exceptional cases notwithstanding, it remains true that people's use of language in seventeenth- and eighteenth-century England correlated directly with their position in society. The best evidence for this is David Cressy's wide-ranging study of literacy in England from 1580 to 1730. "The hierarchy of social rank in pre-industrial England is precisely and vividly illuminated" by data on what percentage of different classes were able to sign their names to wills, marriage licenses, and depositions for ecclesiastical courts (118). Cressy's book establishes or confirms a number of premises that are crucial to chapters 1 and 2 below. He shows, for example, that British society of the period could be "clustered" in terms of illiteracy into high, middle, and low: clergy and gentry almost 100 percent literate (except for the women); trades- and craftspeople, merchants, servants, and yeomen in the middle with literacy rates from 20 to 80 percent; and laborers almost 100 percent illiterate. His data, drawn from more than twenty thousand depositions and other records, reveal a clear difference in literacy between Londoners and everyone else, suggesting that speech communities were more likely to retain low-class features outside the capital than in. Literacy increased significantly in the Restoration and early eighteenth century: women were 90 percent illiterate, or more, until 1660, but had improved to 50 percent illiterate by 1750; men made less progress from about 70 percent illiteracy in 1640 to 55 percent in 1715. These figures are compatible with a significantly increased awareness of standards of correctness in English in the eighteenth century.

A much fuller introduction of literary, linguistic, and historical contexts for this book would be possible, and perhaps interesting, but unnecessary if my conclusions are as uncontroversial as I believe they are. Let me turn now to a survey, so brief as to be only a sample in some cases, of what has been written so far on the subject.

Twentieth-century relations between language and social class have been studied in some depth, most ably and successfully by William Labov. Labov introduced new methods of eliciting informal, unprepared speech from urban and rural working-class informants and has shown in dozens of ways (that have in turn been replicated and confirmed in dozens of different speech communities here and abroad) that the syntax and pronunciation of working-class people differ systematically from standard English. All students of English deserve to know his work, including a brilliant little experiment on correlations between pronunciation of the letter *r* and three strata of social class in New York City department stores. More importantly, the work of Labov and his colleagues has made it difficult not to approach language as a context-dependent mode of human behavior.[2]

Some of my ideas on relations between language and social class in the eighteenth century have been anticipated by K. C. Phillipps (1969) and Joan Platt (1926). Otherwise, very little has been written on this topic, except perhaps in analysis of the literary contexts for lower-class and upper-class language.

It seems reasonable to believe that the unadorned, plain prose styles that gained literary popularity in the late seventeenth century have more in common with lower-class language than with courtly styles. Members of the Royal Society attacked the excessive complexity of some prose styles that had recently been fashionable, and advocated a "close, naked, natural" way of writing. On the other hand, very few authors, no matter what their rank in society, re-

9

stricted themselves exclusively to plain prose, and the choice of high style or low was usually made on the basis of genre, not social class. Dryden, a founding member and leading spirit of the Royal Society committee on language (1664–65), eschews the more exotic flowers of rhetoric in much of his prose but writes courtly dedications when he needs to, and the *Essay of Dramatic Poesy* (1668), though it refers approvingly to progress in "arts and sciences" that has accompanied the labors of the Royal Society, is in no respect a proletarian text. Addison, considered a master of the middle style, wrote high-flown, majestic oriental allegories. Justice has not been done to the abundance and variety of un-plain, high, splendid prose in the Restoration and eighteenth century.

The literary qualities of what seems to be lower-class language in plays and novels have received attention. Any full appreciation of Bunyan and Defoe demands a commensurate appreciation of colloquial, "ordinary" English (as in Watt, 1957). Two of the best books on English style deal with artful disorderliness in the language of Ben Jonson's comedy and "creatural" reality in the language of Shakespeare's dramas (see Barish and Auerbach, respectively), but both are more concerned with literary conventions of the lower genres than with social class. Neither the Ciceronians nor the Senecans in Morris Croll's scheme for seventeenth-century prose have lower-class origins or values.

When we look for research on language appropriate to upper-class English men and women, we find a German monograph on the history of courtly vocabulary in French (Krings, 1961) and several helpful studies of courtly language in the fourteenth century or thereabouts. I have profited from essays by William Wimsatt, W. J. Bate, Richard Ohmann, and Geoffrey Leech, each of whom in a different way has forwarded our understanding and appreciation of complexity in the syntax of literary prose. Irvin Ehrenpreis has a lovely article on the artfulness with which Swift mixes high and low styles, and David Lodge (52–56) writes sensibly about stylistics, what it can do and what it cannot.

NOTES

1. For examples of low, vulgar language in the Countess of Stafford and Lady Sarah Lennox, and of oaths, bad spelling, and bad grammar in gentlefolk and educated people, see William Matthews, "Polite Speech in the Eighteenth Century" (1937), and the *Verney Letters*, 1:189.

Introduction

2. See William Labov, *Sociolinguistic Patterns*, and Peter Trudgill, *The Social Differentiation of English in Norwich* (1974). Basil Bernstein's research, though provocative and substantial, has been attacked for failing to understand that lower-class or nonwritten language may be just as sophisticated as middle-class, educated language (see Burton Hatlen, "The Quest for the Concrete Particular" [1979]). The usefulness of Bernstein's assumptions is apparent in Paul Kay, "Language Evolution and Speech Style" (1977), but it should be amended to take account of context (see Jewson, Sachs, and Rohner, "The Effect of a Narrative Context" [1981]). A number of learned journals now follow the progress of research in this area, for example *Language in Society* or the *International Journal of the Sociology of Language*.

CHAPTER ONE

Lower-Class English, 1660–1800

T HE WORKING hypothesis of this chapter is that lower-class English in the eighteenth century has three mutually inter-dependent traits: colloquialism, incorrectness, and old-fashioned-ness. *Colloquialisms* are linguistic features that occur commonly in spoken, informal English, and rarely in written, formal English. *In-correctness* in English depends on who has decided what is correct and what is not; in this case, it can be defined by the canons of correctness that were evolving from 1650 on, as codified by Robert Lowth, Samuel Johnson, George Campbell, and Henry Home, Lord Kames, after 1750. *Old-fashioned* locutions, for purposes of this study, are those that were current in Shakespeare's lifetime but had lapsed from favor by about 1700.

What gives special point to these three large headings—collo-quialism, solecism, and archaism—is that they are precisely what the more elegant and refined speakers and writers of the time were trying to avoid. The first traces of neoclassicist and prescriptivist ideals for elegance and refinement may be found long before 1660, in Ben Jonson for example (*Timber*, 33–42). John Dryden's *Essay of Dramatic Poesy* (1668) serves quite nicely as a test of these criteria for vulgarity. It was written at the outset of our period, for an upper-class readership, to defend English literary culture. Dryden com-posed it and revised it with fastidious care. The effect of about 80 percent of his revisions for the second edition of 1684 is to make his language less colloquial, more correct, or more up-to-date. The *Essay* is not entirely typical of Dryden's prose (he is more chatty and informal in later prefaces), nor is it overpoweringly aristocratic in style (it is not as courtly as the Earl of Chesterfield, not as urbane and refined as Horace Walpole's letters), but it shows us a writer ac-tively distancing himself from lower-class norms, and so provides an opposite end to what then becomes a sociolinguistic spectrum of language.

Part I of this chapter discusses some of the problems of finding examples of lower-class English from the ages that preceded the age of tape recorders, and uses carefully selected texts as a basis for the colloquialism/solecism/archaism hypothesis. It turns then to *Moll Flanders*, ostensibly written by a very low-class person, and quotes a fairly large number of passages from a relatively small number of pages to show in some detail the different ways in which Moll's language is colloquial, incorrect, and archaic. In part II I list assumptions about language and social class that allow us to think of these three traits as class-related. The social significance of Dryden's revisions in the *Essay* comes into focus within broader movements toward refinement and away from vulgarity; Swift and Pope carry on where Dryden left off. Part III examines eighteenth-century grammars that clearly defined standards for formal correctness in English. Their examples, as well as their precepts, suggest that the English writing public did not consciously connect solecism with colloquialism, archaism, and social vulgarity until about 1760 or 1770.

I. TEXTS

Examples of authentic lower-class English might be drawn from the following categories of texts: those written for lower-class readers, on the theory that such readers would prefer language they were familiar with; those written about lower-class people, on the theory that characters in such texts would speak as they speak in real life; or those written by lower-class people, on the theory that their writings will display clear signs of their class origin. These three categories overlap, of course. The first two, however, cannot be depended on, and the third is problematic.

A large part of what was written explicitly for a lower-class readership in the seventeenth and eighteenth centuries was religious or political. Very little of this makes concessions to a poorly educated readership, either in style or in content. Best-sellers by William Penn (1693/1718), Bernard Mandeville (1714), William Pulteney (1726), William Law (1728), Joseph Butler (1736), George Whitefield (1740), John Wesley (1743), "Junius" (1769), John Howard (1777), and Thomas Paine (1791) give no indication of having adopted the language of hoi polloi. Even if a given author seems to be assuming lower-class points of view and imitating lower-class style (as Swift and John Arbuthnot may have done in satirical or polemical writings), that is no help because we have no criteria for judging how successful the imitation is.

Literary writings (in contrast to religious or political writings) may seem a more promising source for samples of the English of the uneducated mob. But it is hard to identify with confidence any substantial literary text that has not been shaped and molded by the conventions that attach to the genre it exemplifies; literature imitates literature as often as it does life. For example, look at *The London Spy* (1698), a popular (fictitious) tour guide to the sights and sounds of the London underworld by Ned Ward, a tavern-keeper of lower-class origins. Of this book its first modern editor wrote, "Coarse it undoubtedly is. . . . Its author, however, belonged to the people, and wrote primarily for them" (par. 2). But the first three sentences of *The London Spy* make rambunctious allusion to Diogenes, Socrates, Aristotle, Virgil, and Descartes. Ward's prevailing tone is mock-pedantic as well as vulgar. The book falls squarely within a family of Renaissance genres grouped by Frank Chandler as "anatomies of roguery": beggar-books (most popular in the early sixteenth century); cony-catching pamphlets (the tricks of London con men and pickpockets, all the rage in the 1590s); and prison tours (from 1600). Even its title is a literary allusion, to Giovanni Marana's *Turkish Spy* (1684; transl. 1687; see Beasley, 46–49). One of the first sights of the town that Ward introduces us to is a beggar:

> As soon as we came near the Bar, a thing started up all Ribbon, Lace and Feathers, and made such a Noise with her Bell and her Tongue together, that had half a dozen Paper-Mills been at Work within three Yards . . . (3),

which may easily be modeled after John Donne's courtier in *Satyre* IV,

> Towards me did runne
> A thing more strange, then on Niles slime, the Sunne
> E'r bred. . . . Yet I must be content
> With his tongue, in his tongue call'd complement:
> In which he can win widdowes, and pay scores . . . ,

itself a version of Horace's toad-eating bore in *Satire* I, ix. If Donne and Horace seem too poetic to serve as models, the usurer and the cit in Thomas Nashe's *Pierce Penilesse* (1592) will do almost as well

(30–31). There is no doubt that Ward was trying to appeal to a popular readership, that is, to sell as many copies of his book as possible, but the language of *The London Spy* derives more from literary than from authentic lower-class sources.

There are similar difficulties in texts written about lower-class people—literary servants and hostlers and thieves are just as likely to be imitated from earlier works of literature as from flesh and blood. Rowdy servants of Restoration and eighteenth-century comedy may go back to roister-doisters of the Elizabethan stage, or to medieval Vices, or to their prototypes in Plautus. Rascals of prose fiction and popular biography and travel books in the late seventeenth century and early eighteenth are based on their predecessors in earlier literary texts, not so far as is known on reality. According to Frank Chandler, *The English Rogue* (1665) uses episodes from *The Caterpillers of this Nation Anatomized* (1659), which itself refurbishes some of the same anecdotes and jests from Clavell's *Recantation of an ill led Life* (1628) that will reappear in the book on *Street-Robberies Consider'd* (1728) that has been attributed to Defoe (Chandler, 114–15; E. Baker, 2:126–34). If this process of literary imitation has happened in one case, how can we know that it has not happened in others, or in all?

The problem with texts written by lower-class people is that it is hard to be confident that even the least educated among authors have not acquired some refinement by reading. A small degree of literacy opens up inexhaustible treasures of literary culture. We have seen how thoroughly the commoner Ned Ward must have assimilated the literary conventions of satire. I believe that most of the fiction written by relatively uneducated writers is if anything more derivative, more clearly modeled after well-known literary exemplars, than other fiction is. An eighteenth-century chapbook was cited, several pages back, to illustrate the way fiction designed for poor and poorly educated readers is inhabited by characters from chivalric romance. Passages from another chapbook suggest that the language of these popular narratives may be equally high-flown. 'It is life or death, fair Phillis, I look for, let me not languish in despair, give Judgment, O ye fair, give Judgment, that I may know my doom; a word from thy sacred lips can cure a bleeding heart" (Ashton, 143). These are supposedly the words of the son of a servant, "meanly born," in a chapbook published by Cluer Dicey in London (probably 1710–40).

The first step in selecting useful texts, then, is to confine oneself to nonliterary documents, produced without plans for publication, by people with a minimum of formal education. Plans for publication, however tentative, may be presumed to affect a document's correctness and formality. A lower-grade clerk making notes for his own record-keeping purposes would have been less likely to prettify his language or edit his own natural style than the same clerk preparing copy for an official publication. A steward on a country estate writing hurriedly to his employer about the progress of routine repairs and seasonal farm operations would have had less temptation to strike literary poses than any writer of "familiar letters" during the century following Voiture and Mme. de Sévigné. Documents like these (they are relatively rare) may serve as a minimal empirical base for a model of lower-class language in the eighteenth century.

Here follow twenty quotations, dating from 1697 to approximately 1830, from nonliterary texts that no one thought about publishing for roughly two hundred years: manuscript notes by a minor parliamentary clerk, the journal of an obscure merchant, letters of lower servants, a rural Methodist's narrative of persecution, and the autobiographical memoir of a Quaker brought up as a farmer's boy. They have survived almost by accident and have been dragged into the light of day by historians and editors catering to the twentieth century's insatiable appetite for primary sources of almost any sort. Since they are brief, and since the solecisms, colloquialisms, and archaisms they embody are commonplace, they do not prove a theory, but they can support a hypothesis; they are samples of the kind of usage that might distinguish lower-class from standard eighteenth-century English.

How do we know that a particular word or phrase was considered incorrect in the eighteenth century? or colloquial? or archaic? These questions will be asked again and answered in more detail below, with texts from Defoe and Dryden for illustration. In this preliminary run-through of a line of reasoning that will be more fully developed a few pages further on, I identify solecisms by referring briefly to Robert Lowth's *Short Introduction to English Grammar* (1762), the most influential of the major prescriptive grammars, and to George Campbell's *Philosophy of Rhetoric* (1776), for certain details.

About half of Lowth's rules are aimed at solecisms that were also archaisms: they had been perfectly acceptable in 1600, as can be indicated by quotation from Shakespeare. If the *Oxford English*

Dictionary (*OED*) cannot furnish examples of a particular usage later than the seventeenth century, if the same usage is now obsolete but was current in Shakespeare, that usage also may be considered archaic. To identify archaisms of syntax I depend on standard histories of English by Barbara Strang and Albert Baugh.

Colloquialisms are at once easier and harder to put a label to: easier because our own judgment has some authority to tell us which expressions do not belong in formal written texts, though they may sound perfectly natural in informal speech; harder because eighteenth-century grammarians were not as interested in marking colloquialisms as in castigating solecisms. Eric Partridge's *Dictionary of Slang and Unconventional English* and the *OED* are of material assistance here.

First, four quotations from *The Minute Book of James Courthope.* *The Minute Book* is not a book at all but a manuscript from which the official report of a parliamentary committee was to be compiled, "after which it must usually have been destroyed" (according to its modern editor, p. v)—this being the only such document that has survived from the seventeenth and eighteenth centuries. Courthope was one of four clerks who petitioned the House of Commons for more pay in 1711. In 1696 his salary was twenty-five guineas a year, plus thirty pounds in fees. Nothing else is known of him.

(1) 1697: "They should never have such another opportunity, for that there was a Regiment of Irish comeing" (19): *for that* used as a subordinate conjunction to mean 'because' is an archaism. It is not in Johnson's *Dictionary* (or, for that matter, in the *OED*), but it is ordinary and acceptable usage in Shakespeare: "you malign our senators for that / They are not such as you" (*Coriolanus*, I, i, 113); "Do not extort thy reasons for this cause, / For that I woo" (*Twelfth Night*, III, i, 153).

(2) 1698: "noe tickets is to be paid till La. Day" (30): a solecism, by Lowth's rules, which prescribe that in correct English "the Verb agrees with the [subject in] Nominative Case in number and person" (97). This particular solecism may be considered an archaism also, in that Elizabethan writers seem to have been less concerned about subject-verb agreement than Lowth was (Strang, 146). "The houses he makes lasts till doomsday" (*Hamlet*, V, i, 59). "The posture of your blows are yet unknown" (*Julius Caesar*, V, i, 33).

(3) 1698: "the parson shall be lyable to a fine which marryes anyone without produces a certificate" (31). *Without* as a subordinate conjunction, rather than as a preposition, is archaic; we would

say 'unless'. Shakespeare has "not without the prince be willing" (*Much Ado*, III, iii, 80). *Which* was used to refer to persons in Shakespeare's time, as in the Lord's Prayer: "Our Father, which art in Heaven" (1611 translation). But by 1762 this usage had been condemned: "*which* is used of things only" (Lowth, 133). There are two more solecisms in this sentence: the relative pronoun is separated from its antecedent (Campbell, 219–22), and the subject of the verb "produces" is omitted (Lowth, 122).

(4) 1698: "Mr Wilson appeared and offered another Clause in lieu of that which he offered before" (25): a solecism—the rules for sequence of tenses (Lowth, 118ff.) call for the second verb to be 'had offered', not 'offered'.

Francis Rogers, the son of a Thames Street grocer, made his living as a merchant, but in manuscript journals that were not published till 1936 he confesses to "the itch of roving" (199). The next four quotations are drawn from his handwritten "Brief Observations of the Most remarkable Occurences that hapn'd in a Voyage To the East Indies. Began November 20th: 1701."

(5) 1701 and 1704: "The weather indifferent fair" (143); "a mighty fragrant smell" (146); "generally calm and prodigious hot" (227). Shakespeare had no scruples about omitting the -*ly* on an adverb modifying an adjective: "It is indifferent cold," says Osric (*Hamlet*, V, ii, 96); "excellent well"; "plaguy proud."

(6) 1702: "We had a strong boarded awning over the Quarter Deck, which it tore away smack smooth" (145). Eric Partridge lists "smack-smooth" as "colloquial until the late 19th century, then dialectal"; the *OED* cites Smollett's translation of *Don Quixote* in 1755 as the earliest known example.

(7) 1702: "they pretended that we were going a-pirating" (147). Verb phrases that use the prefix *a-* with the present participle ("to go a-hunting"; "they fell a-laughing") served many of the same purposes in Shakespeare's lifetime as progressive forms do now (*be* plus verb -*ing*). The modern progressive forms were still evolving during the seventeenth and eighteenth centuries. As late as 1837 the *North American Review* branded the passive progressive ("is being asked") as "an outrage upon English idiom" (Baugh, 353–54). "A-verb-ing" expressions, then, could be considered archaic, colloquial, and incorrect, all three.

(8) 1704: "There was no great search made after him now, nor we heard no more of him" (207). The double negative here is an archaism (Strang, 152)—or is it something less exotic, a mere slip of

the pen? Did Rogers start to write, 'nor did we hear more of him' and switch half way through into 'but we heard no more of him'? If so, we can attribute to this sentence just the sort of sloppiness that is most characteristic of speech, not writing, so it may count as a colloquialism.

The next five quotations are from letters written in the course of daily business by lower servants or tradespeople or craftsmen attached to the households of country estates. Almost all such letters have perished, because in most people's opinion they were not worth preserving; they survive mostly in more inclusive collections of family papers.

(9) 1721: "I do not know of anything else to do except you please to have the harth in the kitching mended." (10) 1759: "We'd advise you to have the glass all slated & fixed in the frames with puttie they are much neater than to be put in with lead & turns rain much better." The first of these, identified in *The Letters and Papers of the Banks Family of Revesby Abbey* (74) as by William Burbidge, servant to Joseph Banks, employs an archaic subordinate conjunction, *except*, meaning 'unless'. The second, by William Perfed (237), exemplifies different kinds of sloppiness from quotation 8 above, false conjunction and imperfect agreement: it was probably intended to mean that 'they are much neater than frames put in with lead and turn rain much better'. We may choose to think of such usages either as violations of grammatical rules or as the natural discontinuities of colloquial English.

(11) 1730: "Hee tould mee hee would bee oute a boute May day next and desiread of mee to aquant you with it and that hee would cale of mee for an aser at that time" (*Banks Papers*, 117). In standard English: 'He told me that he would be out about May Day next and desired me to acquaint you with that fact and said that he would call me for an answer at that time'. There are four features, not counting spelling, that have had to be changed to translate this sentence into the standard English of the educated middle class: the function word *that* has been inserted (Lowth, 145); two extraneous particles or prepositions have been removed (Campbell, 158); pronominal reference has been clarified (Lowth, 138 n. 2); and a nonparallel construction—"aquant you with it and that hee would cale"—has been rewritten (Lowth, 117 n. 2).

(12) 1752: "I told her I wold not Lett it for no tirm under 21 years. She was in a great passion and said it was all along of me" (*Shardeloes Papers*, 112). Here Ambrose Nickson, a steward, writes

to his master about negotiations with a tenant. *Along of*—'owing to': a solecism or dialectal usage in the nineteenth century, according to Eric Partridge.

(13) 1790: "My Lord I should be Glad if you please to send me a pound of Silk to mend the Covy nets for I used all the Silk I have, for theay are tore very much and so are the Silk flews allso. . . . I think it will be hard to me, to save the birds and he goe and kill them; he may if he please go along with me a shooting. . . . My Lord, they have don a mowing in the Park. . . . there wants nothing moor to Be don to it but the two windows to be lathed" (*Verney Letters*, 2:300–301). The first sentence of this, a letter from a Mr. Jack White to Earl Verney, illustrates what might be called the *over-concatenation* characteristic of a great deal of colloquial discourse: 'I am X, if you send Y, for I used Z, for they are P, and so are Q'. *And* meaning 'if' in the second sentence is an archaism, as are "a shooting" and "a mowing" further on. Elizabethan English gave freer play to the use of impersonals ("there wants nothing moor") than eighteenth-century English did.

Turn now to *The Case of John Nelson* (1745), a narrative "Written by Himself" to demonstrate God's providence in a world most inhospitable to Methodists. Nelson was "as able to get my Living with my Hands, as any Man of my Trade in England" (5), but that is all we know of his social standing. The story of his impressment into the army by a malicious alehousekeeper, on the grounds that "several" of his townsfolk "did not like so much preaching," is shored up at every joint and corner with biblical quotations but shows no other signs of literary influence. This document is probably an exception to our rule concerning intention to publish, for Nelson wrote to vindicate himself and to inculpate his persecutors. But publication in Nelson's case was not a literary or cultural event; it was a means to a religious end. Perhaps he wrote in the same manner as he preached: "I do not study what to say, but speak as the Spirit of God enables me" (35).

(14) 1745: "Then Mr. *Brooke* laid the Petitions before them, sent by my neighbouring Gentlemen, which testified I had done no Evil, but had behaved myself well in my Neighbourhood, and had always maintained my Family very well; and they desired them to set me at Liberty" (4). Nelson omits *that* in indirect discourse (see comments on quotation 11 above) and mixes up pronominal reference in the last clause (Lowth, 138; Campbell, 219, 223).

(15) 1745: "You have given me such a Character, as not an-

other Man in *England* will that knows me"; "the Dungeon is a loath-some Place as ever I saw" (7); a poor man "all the Cloathes upon whose Back were not worth one Shilling, neither did they lay any Thing to his Charge" (7). These three sentences exemplify lower-class habits of asseveration or emphatic assertion. The first two might be classified as colloquial: 'as X as any in England'; 'as X as ever I saw'. The third exploits Elizabethan flexibilities of word order for emphasis: 'X was not Y, neither was it Z'. On page 9 Nelson has, "the lovingest People that ever I saw in my Life." These particular forms of asseveration will not be found in formal eighteenth-century texts.

(16) 1745: "for they did bridle their Tongues in my Presence" (13). Polite eighteenth-century authors omitted the "pleonastic *do*": 'they bridled'. But in Shakespeare, "I have forgot why I did call thee back" (*Romeo and Juliet*, II, ii, 170).

The last document in this list was probably written in the 1830s. Its author, Joseph Jewell (1763–1846), had published a number of pamphlets and poems during the years 1801 to 1844, having worked his way out of blue-collar lower-class London to middle-class prosperity as an industrial chemist. This, his *Autobiographical Memoir*, however, comes down to us as a manuscript composed with "little attention to punctuation [or spelling] and none to paragraphing" (113). If Jewell, a highly intelligent man, intended publication, he must either have made a conscious decision not to try to produce the kind of standard English that a publisher or editor would have expected, or he tried and failed; in either case the language of the memoir seems suitable to the son of a "horse dealer and also a little farmer" (126), whose education circa 1770–76 suffered from "being so often taken away [from school] to work," and not to Jewell's later flourishing status as commercial chemist. At thirteen years of age, Jewell left home for full-time employment (up to seventeen hours a day) as hostler, farmer, carter, shoemaker, porter.

(17)1830(?): "the next circomstance that comes to my reccollection is, my father being going to a fair and ordered me and my brother to pick some stones off an acre of clover" (127). It is hard to describe exactly what is happening in the syntax of this sentence ("my father being going . . . and ordered"), but it certainly is not formal, correct, up-to-date written English.

(18) 1830(?): "My master and I was toping up a haystack" (132). Plural subject, singular verb.

(19) 1830(?): "B. S[tacy] returned a note and some of their article which they had made and had sold the same sort to their customers" (145). The writer here expresses himself perfectly clearly but never stops to sort out his relative pronouns as Lowth and Campbell would have wanted him to.

(20) 1830(?): "It seemed as if they could not invent oaths bad enough, and yet bad as they were, they were catching, for I having been in the habbit of swearing from an early age, and very bad when in a passion, was apt to make use of the same shocking oaths as I was so frequently hearing, and beside this specie of iniquity, their conversation, when a number of them got togeather, was obsene and corrupting" (154). Vivid, true to life, and overconcatenated, in the manner that urgent or hurried speech tends to be.

Having borrowed from widely scattered documents to establish a basis for the major hypothesis of this chapter, we are entitled now to look at a single text where linguistic features detailed by this hypothesis dominate the overall texture of the prose, *Moll Flanders* (1722). Daniel Defoe, of course, made "determined efforts to establish himself in society as a gentleman," and "gave expression to his ideas on the subject of gentility" at great length on many occasions. He was an accomplished craftsman, with a goodly repertoire of literary styles. My subject here, however, is the most vulgar of Defoe's many voices.[1] Quotations will be grouped under each of the three principal categories of usage in turn.

Colloquialisms

Colloquialisms are either homely, idiomatic expressions, unsuitable to formal academic prose, or constructions that belong to spoken rather than to written discourse. As it manifests itself in speech, any natural language differs in structure from the same language in normal written form; it is, for example, more redundant and more disjunctive. Word order is freer. The word *colloquialism* may refer as often to these structural features as to particular words or phrases.

Catch phrases, proverbial sayings, and clichés that unliterary folk might use in everyday speech are common in Moll's narrative:

there is no great Bustle in putting an end to a Poor bodies family. (16)

when I ask'd the Daughter for it, she huft me. (16)

I had enough to do to come away. (16)

the Children of it had no more to do but just stay at home. (16)

they had no more to say to me, than to Jest with me. (16)

however she stood upon her Legs, as they say. (197)

seeing the Coast clear. (197)

the Woman that had him was easie. (198)

I had some things that were Monies worth. (198)

I had not so much as a Lodging to go to, or a bit of Bread to Eat. (17)

they that had me, wou'd not part with me; and as for me, tho' I shou'd have been very well Treated with any of the other, yet I could not be better than where I was. (18)

A Circumstance . . . which put me to my Shifts. (30)

We would not expect to find expressions like these in the mouths of courtiers or university graduates.

This list, which could be extended almost indefinitely, does not include criminal language; real thieves' cant is so rare in *Moll Flanders* as to be anomalous. Paragraph two of the novel has Moll's comrades "gone out of the World by the Steps and the String" (7), but that slangy locution is not part of the specialized jargon of highwaymen, cant in its narrowest sense, which was supposed to be incomprehensible to outsiders. There is a short lexicon of thieves' cant in *The English Rogue* (1665): *Autem Mort*, 'a married woman'; *Abram*, 'naked'; *Bughar*, 'a cur'; *Bouse*, 'drink'. Perhaps "Mother Midnight" (162, 381) is a cant expression, appearing in Francis Grose's *Dictionary of the Vulgar Tongue* (1785) as 'a midwife'. The infrequency of such expressions suggests, however, that Moll's language belongs to a generalized lower class, rather than to some rougher stratum of society.[2]

The language of asseveration in *Moll Flanders* is noticeably unsophisticated and pettybourgeois:

it would not be proper, no, not tho' a general Pardon should be issued, even without Exceptions. (7)

nor can I give the least Account how I was kept alive. (8)

and left me about Half a Year old; and in bad Hands you may be sure. (8)

and it made Mirth enough among them, you may be sure. (12)

nay, says she, the Child may come to be a Gentlewoman for ought any body knows, she has a Gentlewoman's Hand, says she; this pleas'd me mightily you may be sure. (13)

This was prudently manag'd enough. (16)

and with a glad Heart you may be sure. (17)

After he had thus baited his Hook, and found easily enough the Method. (20)

for I had never had the least thought of what she expected. (21)

His Words . . . put me in Disorder enough. (22)

telling me . . . abundance of such fine things. (24)

I was cunning enough, not to give the least room to any in the Family to suspect me. (26)

There is something chatty and comfortable about these emphatic phrases, but they would not suit an upper-middle-class drawing room or a gentlewoman's salon.

A less familiar feature of colloquial prose is discourse signaling, of which Moll uses at least three kinds. Discourse signals are words or phrases whose function is not to make reference, as common and proper nouns usually do, and not to make attributions or predications, as do most adjectives and verbs, but to call attention to a direction or turn or stage just taken or reached at that point in a linear sequence of messages.[3] *Nevertheless* is a discourse signal commonly found in educated English but not in Moll Flanders, who prefers expressions like "in short," "*viz.*," "nay," "as they say," "well," "I say." The phrase "in short" as Moll uses it seldom summarizes in concise form, as its lexical meaning proclaims it will; rather, it signals the climax of a series that has had little or no shape to it up to that point:

I had no Policy in all this, you may easily see it was all Nature, but it was joyn'd with so much Innocence, and so much Passion, That in short, it set the good Motherly Creature a weeping too. (12)

and a great many fine Things have been said of Mrs. *Betty*, I assure you; and particularly, that she is the Handsomest young Woman in *Colchester*; and, in short, they began to Toast her Health in the Town. (20)

It was his younger Sisters Chamber, that I was in, and as there was no Body in the House, but the Maids below Stairs, he was it may be the ruder: In short, he began to be in Earnest with me indeed; perhaps he found me a little too easie, for God knows [etc.]. (23)

Some of Defoe's most characteristic verbal mannerisms may be read better as discourse signals than as independent lexical items. "As they say," "*viz.*," and similar phrases recur so often and sometimes, it appears, so unnecessarily that their main function may be simply to interrupt the flow, calling attention to what precedes and follows them:

He began with that unhappy Snare to all Women, (*viz.*) taking Notice upon all Occasions how pretty I was, as he call'd it; how agreeable, how well Carriaged, and the like; and this . . . (19)

I must say, that if such a prospect of Work had presented it self at first, when I began to feel the approach of my miserable Circumstances; I say, had such a prospect of getting my Bread . . . (202)

and so led the Child on again: Here, I say, the Devil put me upon killing the Child. (194)

"I say" has the additional effect of reestablishing the speaker's presence and heightening a sense of social immediacy, somewhat as "you know" does in twentieth-century colloquial English.

More obviously colloquial kinds of discourse signals are the preliminary and resumptive talk-words which are common in spoken English but rare in written English, *well, nay, what, why*:

and I should not go to Service till I was bigger. Well, this did not Satisfie me. (11)

Great, Rich, and High, and I know not what. Well, after Mrs. *Mayoress* was gone . . . (13)

I would certainly have carried the things back again; but that went off after a while: Well, I went to Bed for that Night. (193)

so that I was mightily made of, as we say; nay, and they were not a little Angry. (17)

my Heart spoke as plain as a Voice, that I lik'd it; nay, when ever he said . . . (22)

Many such words crop up in dialogue in *Moll Flanders*, where they seem quite at home:

Well, Madam forsooth, says she . . . ? what, will you do it by your Fingers Ends? . . . Why, what can you Earn. (11)

Why, can you live without Victuals? . . . Well, Mrs. —— says the *Mayoress* . . . Well Miss says she. (12)

Disconcertingly, they also crop up in the conversation of people who Defoe tells us are landed gentry, where they seem quite incongruous. Moll's first husband's genteel family josh and jibe together in exactly the same phrases as Moll and Mother Midnight later on:

Why Sister . . . Ay, and . . . Well, well . . . Why Madam . . . Prethee Child. (43)

Well, *says the Mother*, then . . . Why but Child . . . Why then Madam . . . Nay. (44)

Come then, *says she* . . . Why first, *says I*, . . . Ay, *says I* with all my Heart. (175)

As to that, says the *Governess* . . . Why, *said I* . . . Well, well, *says my Governess*. (176)

The third group of discourse signals common in *Moll Flanders* may be classified as different forms of topicalization. *Topic* is "what you are talking about"; it is *known* information, not *new* information, and tends in ordinary discourse to appear near the beginning of a sentence. Sometimes the topic is the same as the grammatical subject, but not always, and a string of sentences may have the same topic but different subjects. Some sentences do not have topics at all. In English, the commonest way of signaling topic is an *as for* or *as to* phrase:

> As for my Money I gave it all to my Mistress Nurse. (13)
>
> I say in every Thing except Honesty; and for that, tho' this was a Lady most exactly Just . . . (17)
>
> But as to Dancing they could hardly help my learning Country Dances. (18)
>
> His Brother was out of Town; and as for his Father, he had been at *London*. (23)
>
> as for the Gold I spent whole Hours in looking upon it. (26)
>
> as for my Gentleman, he staid out as he told me he would. (29)

Topicalization appears more frequently in colloquial English than in written English because it is a way of explicitly changing, or drawing attention to, the topic to be discussed. A primitive way of accepting a topic in conversation is to repeat it, throw it back in the speaker's face:

> But what shall I do now, *says I*, must not I carry it again? Carry it again! *says she*, Ay, if you are minded to be sent to *Newgate*. (200)
>
> Why are you merry, *says I*? the Story has not so much Laughing room in it, as you imagine; I am sure I have had a Pack of ugly Rogues. *Laugh*, says my Governess, I laugh Child to see what a lucky Creature you are. (248)

This gambit of repeating the words that one wishes to comment on is common in John Bunyan, whose socioeconomic stratum was several layers lower than Defoe's.

The last in our list of colloquial traits in Defoe's book counts as colloquial mainly because of its informality, its helter-skelterness. It shows an absence of the particular form of organization called *focus*, which is the converse of topic, and which appears in ordinary discourse at the end of a sentence in English as *new* information. A good periodic sentence has strong end-focus. Many of Defoe's sentences seem unperiodic in the extreme; they have no single focus at all but proceed in apparently haphazard fashion, adding one clause to the last until for no special reason they stop:

> but then I was come to be so good a Workwoman myself, and the Ladies were so kind to me, that it was plain I could maintain myself, that is to say, I could Earn as much for my Nurse as she was able by it to keep me; so she told them, that if they would give her leave, she would keep the Gentlewoman as she call'd me, to be her Assistant, and teach the Children, which I was very well able to do; for I was very nimble at my Work, and had a good Hand with my Needle, though I was yet very young. (15)

This is the last third of an overconcatenated paragraph that starts with Moll looking now a little "Womanish," *and* also pretty, *so* (i.e., 'therefore') proud; *however*, thrifty, *and* clean, *for* she would wash what she had on were it rags, *but* her nurse would spend her money honestly, *and* tell the ladies what was bought with it, *and* this made them give more, *till*—on and on it goes, tacking one idea onto another in a string of undifferentiated supplements. I have italicized the conjunctions in my paraphrase to stress the miscellaneous character of linkages between one idea or event and the next. We could call such sentences but-and-yet-which chains; they are colloquial because they are apparently unplanned, unordered.

Occasionally in the least elegant passages of *Moll Flanders* we have the feeling that almost any sentence element can be topicalized and lead off sidewise into a new clause, resulting not in a topic chain (a useful and well-organized construction, common in some non-Indo-European languages)[4] but in a chain of topics:

> But my new generous Mistress, for she exceeded the good Woman I was with before, in every Thing, as well as in the matter of Estate; I say in every Thing except Honesty; and for that, tho' this was a Lady most exactly Just, yet I must not forget to say on all Occasions, that the First tho' Poor, was as uprightly Honest as it was possible for any One to be. (17)

(This sentence is of course a fragment; its subject has no predicate.) A favorite jumping-off place for adding new clauses in Defoe is the relative pronoun *which*, used, without particular antecedent, to refer to the idea or event as a whole, that is, *which* used as a conjunction:

> But he did not see his Advantage, which was my happiness for that time. (22)
>
> when his Mother and the young Ladies went Abroad a visiting, which he watch'd so narrowly, as never to miss. (29)

Solecisms

We seem to have modulated gradually into the second major category of linguistic traits, disorderliness and imprecision in grammar and diction. If two of the goals of a good prescriptive grammar are clarity and precision, if such grammars chastise vagueness, ambiguity, or inaccuracy of expression, then several of the colloquialisms described above are also solecisms. More conventional solecisms are also common in *Moll Flanders*, the kind that English teachers are supposed to be busy eradicating:

1. LACK OF PARALLEL CONSTRUCTION

> as my Case came to be known, and that I was too young. (9)
>
> either of Understanding my Case, or how to Amend it. (8)
>
> either to Die, or to the Gallies. (7)
>
> She then talk'd of other things, look'd about into my Accommodations, where was found fault with my wanting Attendance, and Conveniencies, and that I should not be us'd so at her House. (166)
>
> but blotted out the Name, and also the Story about the Dissaster of his Wife, only that she was Dead. (172–73)

2. IMPRECISE PRONOUN REFERENCE

> When any Criminal is condemn'd . . . , if they leave any Children. (7)
>
> but at whose Expence, or by whose Direction I know nothing at all of it. (8–9)

for tho' they sent round the Country to enquire after
them, it seems they could not be found. (9)

many a Woman, who . . . would otherwise be tempted to
Destroy their Children. (168)

In this sentence more than one pronoun is involved:

I had the Advantage of my Ladies, tho' they were my Superiors; but they were all the Gifts of Nature, and which
all their Fortunes could not furnish. (18)

And here the same pronoun refers to two different nominals in two
directions:

yet he offer'd no more all the while we were together,
which was above two Hours, and which I much wonder'd
at. (35)

3. UNNECESSARY REPETITIONS

but not so far, but that I heard all their Discourse, in
which I heard . . . (21)

a Course of Life, which was not only scandalous in itself,
but which in its ordinary Course . . . (8)

except to visit the Lying-Inn Ladies within their Month,
nor then without the old Lady with them. (169)

4. REDUNDANCY (I enclose superfluous words in square brackets)

desir'd I would not give my Consent to his Brother, nor
yet [give him] a flat Denial, but [that I would] hold him in
Suspence a while. (35)

But then came the great and main Difficulty, [and that
was] the Child; this she told me [in so many Words] must
be remov'd, [and that] so [, as] that it should never be possible for any one to discover [it]. (173)

and yet you look fat, and fair Child, says the old Beldam,
and [with that] she stroak'd me over the Face; never be
concern'd Child, *says she*, [going on] in her drolling way; I
have no Murtherers about me: I employ the best and [the]

honestest Nurses [that can be had]; and have as few Children miscarry [under their Hands,] as [there would,] if they were all Nurs'd by Mothers. (174)

Please note that all these examples are drawn from a relatively small number of pages.

Archaisms

Many histories of English and of English prose style assume that the syntax of modern English—with only a few exceptions—was mature and fully ripened by the eighteenth century. Dryden is widely regarded as the first major English prose writer whom we can read as if he were more or less contemporary with us; before Dryden, all English prose has an antiquated flavor. This position needs to be considerably amended,[5] but it gives us a place to start in identifying archaic syntax. If a particular usage is commonplace in Shakespeare, and if histories of the language, including the *OED*, assert that this usage was dying out in the seventeenth century, we can consider it archaic or old-fashioned in 1720.

1. DOUBLE NEGATIVES

I did not know why neither. (12)

I struggled to get away, and yet did it but faintly neither. (22)

she is not so far out of her Senses neither. (46)

You don't know that neither. (20)

Compare *As You Like It*, I, i, 87, "and yet give no thousand crowns neither," or II, ii, 51–52, "this is not Fortune's work neither."

2. ANTIQUATED USE OF AUXILIARIES

In Present-day English, the modal auxiliary *would* usually follows a conditional clause, stated or implied, without much independent meaning; and when it occurs outside the environment of conditional clauses, its primary meaning is 'was accustomed to' (as in, "Every Sunday he would walk to town for a newspaper"). But its primary meaning before 1600 was 'desire to'.

You would ['want to'] be a Gentlewoman. (11)

He was so pleas'd with it, that he would call his Lady. (12)

one of the Ladies took so much Fancy to me, that she would have me Home. (15)

might have had what I would. (26)

Compare *Macbeth*, I, v, 20, "Thou wouldst be great," or *The Comedy of Errors*, IV, iv, 148, "She that would be your wife."[6]

3. A-VERBING CONSTRUCTIONS

This set the old Gentlewoman a Laughing at me. (11)

when he went a Setting. (19)

the young Ladies were all gone a Visiting. (23)

they shan't catch me a Kissing of you. (24)

According to Otto Jespersen, this idiom persists in representation of vulgar speech by nineteenth-century novelists; it is related, in ways that we do not precisely understand, to the evolution of the full range of progressive (periphrastic) tenses.

4. SEQUENCE OF TENSES IN CONDITIONALS AND SUBJUNCTIVES

Had this been the Custom in our Country, I had not been left a poor desolate Girl. (8)

He had stay'd longer with me, but he happen'd to look out. (22)

Had I acted as became me, . . . this Gentleman had either Desisted his Attacks. (25)

A preference for the modern version of this idiom, 'If X had verb-ed, Y *would have* verb-ed', was established during the seventeenth and eighteenth centuries.

5. DATIVES

Elizabethan English accommodated dative or indirect object constructions with a wider variety of verbs than Present-day English does, in different positions:

call'd once or twice for me, to give it me. (17)

just as I had told it her. (51)

she offer'd me to take it herself. (198)[7]

Compare *Troilus*, I, ii, 119, "She came and puts me her white hand to his cloven chin."

6. CONJUNCTIONS

he told me his plain way of Talking had been the Occasion of it, for that he did not make his respect for me so much a Secret. (30)

then I would tell them to remove those Rings, for that I had seen two suspicious Fellows. (196–97)

I was able to do but very little . . . , except it was to run of Errands. (10)

The two texts printed by the *OED* for *except* as a conjunction are both from Shakespeare.

7. ANTITHESES HEAVILY LABELED (remnants or faint traces of euphuism?)

for this young Gentleman as he was plain and Honest, so he pretended to nothing with me, but what was so too. (30)

tho' I had no great Scruples . . . , yet I could not think. (31)

as he did not seem in the least to lessen his Affection to me, so neither did he lessen his Bounty. (31)

as he believed, . . . so he was resolv'd. (31)

But as I easily cou'd see that it would go farther, so I saw likewise . . . (32)

If my searches are representative, there are a good many heavy antitheses in Fielding but none at all in Samuel Johnson; they were dying out during the eighteenth century.

8. RELATIVE PRONOUNS

Before about 1570, *who* and *whom* were still essentially interrogative, and the principal relative was *that*, used alike for people and things.

the little Lass that intends to be a Gentlewoman. (12)

a Woman that mended Lace. (14)

the Mayoress that was. (17)

she having been the first that took any Notice of me. (18)

they that had me. (18)

a gay Gentleman that knew the Town. (19)

Compare *The Taming of the Shrew*, I, i, 77, "players that offer service to your lordship," and I, i, 88, "'twas Soto that your honor means."

9. QUALIFIERS AND INTENSIFIERS

These changed noticeably between 1570 and 1770. The modern reliance on *very, quite,* and *-ly* adverbs is relatively new in the second half of the seventeenth century; before that time, expressions such as *full, right, mighty, grievous, sore,* and *plaguy* were common (Wyld, 391–92):

mighty Grave and Humble. (14)

speaks mighty earnestly. (28)

near half a Year. (29)

this was exceeding kind in her. (15)

I heard abundance of fine things said. (21)

10. AND THAT

This expression is used deictically to gather up previous referents or to introduce a new set of attributes, qualifications, or modifications to what has just been said (see *OED*, s.v. "that," I, 2, a). This idiosyncratic construction should perhaps count as a colloquialism, not an archaism.

I was . . . turn'd out of Doors to the wide World, and that which was still worse, the old honest Woman had two and twenty Shillings of mine. (16)

very willing to be a Servant, and that any kind of Servant they thought fit. (17)

proposes fairly and Honourably to Marry me, and that before he made any other Offer. (29)

34

All those things represented themelves to my View, and that in the blackest and most frightful Form. (174)

11. MISCELLANEOUS

I was a meer Bride all this while (187); like a meer Mother. (15)

Defoe is using *mere* here as Shakespeare does: "The mere perdition of the Turkish fleet" (*Othello*, II, ii, 3), meaning 'utter', 'complete.'

an Inn just against us. (185)
She would have had me let the Maid have waited on me. (178)
he . . . failed not to catch me all alone. (29)

Modern English forms such negatives with auxiliaries, *did not fail.*

I was frighted to Death. (185; another example 180)

Frighted is now rare, according to the *OED*, except when poetic or Scottish; compare Shakespeare, "Find we a time for frighted peace to pant" (*1 Henry IV*, I, i, 2).

on a sudden comes Mrs. *Mayoress.* (12)

Although the *OED* agrees that "on a sudden" is archaic, it gives examples from four nineteenth-century authors, who may, however, be exploiting its old-fashionedness.

prethee, what doest Cry for? (10)
by this and some other of my talk. (13)

Compare *Midsummer Night's Dream*, III, ii, 239, "Wink each at other, hold the sweet jest up." In Present-day English, *other* is an adjective; used as a pronoun it is always plural, except when modified by a quantifier or a determiner such as *any, one, each, the.*

I did indeed cast sometimes with myself what my young Master aim'd at. (15)

This is "cast" in senses 38 and 41 of the *OED*, both obsolete, the latest entries for which are dated 1666 and 1658. Sense 38 gives an example from *Hamlet*, II, i.

> I was tall of my Age. (16)
>
> being forsaken of my Vertue. (29)
>
> thieves . . . who . . . are fain to sell it for a Song. (197)
>
> I warrant ye. (202) She would warrant that *Robin* would tell the Story another way. (51)

The *OED* gives a few later examples of *warrant* in this sense, but they may all be read as conscious archaisms or colloquialisms.

> From this time my Head run upon strange Things. (22)

The *OED* cites examples of *run* as simple past tense (versus *ran*) from 1382 to 1655, one from 1705, and Tennyson's "Northern Farmer."[8]

Students of the English language will recognize that in this section of my argument I have tried to ignore fine points and limit references to standard authorities. This does not mean that there is no room for disagreement about how completely out-of-date or incorrect some of these archaisms and solecisms were in 1721. But brief as it is, my analysis of Moll's language includes approximately two hundred quotations and allusions; they can hardly fail, taken together, to affect the texture of Defoe's prose.

II. Contexts

Each of the three major features of lower-class language is different: archaic English is not necessarily colloquial or sloppy; colloquial English may well be up-to-date and precise; sloppy English (in student essays, for example) is often up-to-the-minute in vocabulary and idiom but formal, stiff, noncolloquial. In the eighteenth century, however, many archaisms were analysed by the grammarians as solecisms, and many of the solecisms most commonly proscribed were archaisms. Both occurred more frequently in colloquial than in written English, and all three have a flavor of the lower classes. This hypothesis is based on the following assumptions about relations of language to social class in the seventeenth and eighteenth centuries:

(1) English that belonged specifically to the lowest ranks in society was colloquial English, spoken not written. At the very bottom of the heap were the utterances of illiterate or barely literate working-class people: chairmen, carters, plowmen, fishwives, ostlers, beggars. This lowest stratum of English overlapped broadly with the next stratum up, but should be distinguished from the language of every sector of the middle class both for reasons of variation (way down the ladder, anything goes—obscenity, slang, dialect, jargon, cant: it is these disreputable elements that Defoe, as editor of Moll's memoirs, assures us he has blue-penciled out of the original), and by its unselfconsciousness—it makes no attempts to be anything other than itself.

(2) Almost as soon as an eighteenth-century English speaker could read, she or he was confronted with notions of correctness and quality in language. Shopkeepers and lower-rank servants might be confined in their everyday existence to English identical to that of illiterate speakers, but they had access to higher dialects, perhaps in school or from their superiors, perhaps through one of the thousands of handbooks and pamphlets sold to the lower middle classes to enable them to become more upper class. That most characteristic of eighteenth-century forms, the periodical essay, owed some of its appeal to frank didacticism on subjects such as manners and genteel behavior and correctness or refinement in language. An awareness of sociolinguistic status was thus imposed on anyone with any education at all, even the most practical one. A liberal education, which taught doctrines of correctness, refinement, and good taste, was always a mark of gentility.

(3) Archaic language survived longer among the lower than among the upper classes. Recent research on the evolution of language proposes that "linguistic variation is the synchronic aspect of linguistic change, and linguistic change is the diachronic aspect of linguistic variation" (Bickerton, 16). In other words, no language changes homogeneously; innovations are never adopted unanimously by all speakers and writers at any one time. Paradoxically, some archaisms and neologisms are always current and always play a part in living speech. But in eighteenth-century England, older forms and idioms lingered longest where academic and social standards had least sway, that is, in the country and among the pro-

letariat. By contrast, and at the opposite extreme, modern, up-to-date English from 1660 to 1800 was educated English. A significant group of men of education and taste worked actively to stamp out the old and cultivate the new.

One can think of counterexamples to most of these premises. It was still true in Defoe's lifetime that aristocrats who had no interest in being courtiers were entitled to be as ignorant as they chose; the "booby squire" was a stock character in drama and fiction. Under the first two Georges a certain segment of the king's own circle took no active interest in English culture. A few overeducated or strong-willed middle-class writers seem to have decided to ignore genteel standards and be as informal as they pleased: Roger L'Estrange, the publicist; Jeremy Collier, the preacher; Richard Bentley, the classical scholar; and George Cheyne, the physician, all write coarse, vigorous, colloquial English.

Some eighteenth-century programs for improving English appear to have been conservative and regressive, not modernist. Swift, in his *Proposal* (1712), designated 1558–1642 as "The Period wherein the *English* Tongue received most Improvement" (17) and set himself self-consciously to reviving elements of the syntax of the King James translation of the Bible (1611) in his own writing (Strang, 1967). Johnson "endeavoured to collect examples and authorities from the writers before the Restoration, whose works" he regarded "as *the wells of English undefiled,* as the pure sources of genuine diction" (*Works,* 5:39). Both writers felt the pull of a "primitivist" nostalgia for a golden age of language (S. Baker, 1980). When it came to the practical business of writing a pamphlet or a dictionary, however, neither Johnson nor Swift embraced obsolete words or discontinued syntactic structures, in substantial numbers, as valid replacements for eighteenth-century words or structures.

At the same time, two strong intellectual or cultural movements that in one way or another influenced the evolution of English, especially educated written English, promoted exactly the kinds of linguistic change that make the language of *Moll Flanders* seem lower class. Prescriptivism in the Restoration and the eighteenth century produced a flood of English grammars—Ian Michael lists and analyzes 273 titles published between 1586 and 1801. Most of them attempted to improve the language in some respects, however speculative or descriptive they may have been in other respects; this almost amounts to a national stampede, which after the union of 1707 definitely included the Scots, in pursuit of correct usage.

Prescriptivism may be subsumed within the other cultural movement I have in mind, neoclassicism itself. Among other things that British neoclassicism valued was a string of un-Flandersean virtues: correctness, elegance, ease, wit, refined taste, gracefulness. In matters linguistic this meant purity and elegance, by which commentators seem in all cases to have intended an English free at least from archaisms and neologisms. Dryden called for "purity of phrase" and "elegance" of language as the "ornaments of peace" in 1679, echoing John Evelyn in 1665 (see Emerson). He was copied in turn by Defoe in 1697, Swift in 1712, and Johnson in 1747. Many of the same phrases occur in all five writers: a longing for "correct," "polished," and "refined" English, a rejection of "barbarity," "corruption," and "cant." People disagreed as to exactly how these ideals could be applied to English, but they could see and had constantly in mind what similar ideals had done for French with the help of practical instructions by Claude Favre de Vaugelas (1647) and others.

And the move to make English more genteel, more correct or precise, and less slangy or vernacular did have some practical consequences. Joseph Addison, in *Spectator* 78, lobbied for *who* and *which*, and made fun of *that* as an all-purpose relative pronoun—in other words, censured the Elizabethan and Defoean use of *that* to refer to people. Swift proudly joined battle for the "Men of Taste," "accomplished" and even "noble" personages of "wit and politeness," against "heavy, illiterate scribblers," "bullies," "footmen," and "pedants" who threatened the citadel of true wit and humour (*Tale of a Tub*, 243–52). In *Tatler* 230 (1710), Swift attacked slovenly, hypermodernist colloquialisms, including contractions ("*I'd h' brot 'um*; but I *han't don't*") and slang (*Phizz, Bamboozle*). In *A Complete Collection of Genteel and Ingenious Conversation, According to the Most Polite Mode and Method Now used At Court* (1738), he ridiculed such colloquialisms as catch phrases and proverbial sayings in the mouths of lords and ladies. Henry Fielding lambasted Colley Cibber's *Apology* for bad writing; in *The Champion* for 29 April 1740, he quotes forty of Cibber's most grievously mangled sentences or phrases and holds them up to ridicule. Pope corrected his private correspondence for publication by excising shirt-sleeve or colloquial locutions in favor of correctness and easy elegance: "go a Raking" becomes "go and see the world," "whom . . . few do justice to" becomes "to whom few will do justice," and "Bayes his entring" becomes "Bayes's entring" (*Correspondence*, 1:128, 138, 261).

The fullest context for this move toward clarity and modernity in language is of course the Enlightenment itself. Voltaire damned every work of literature "that is not equally clear, chaste, and simple" (212). Shaftesbury praised "Attic elegance" and refinement and correctness at the expense of "rudeness" and "barbarity" (151, 141); at one point in *Advice to an Author* (1710) he seems to welcome "etymologists, philologists, grammarians" to the task of exposing "bombast in style" (156). It is not just third-rate authors who appear in Pope's *Dunciad*: Defoe is held up to contempt merely because he was a prolific lower-class dissenter, and William Caxton merely because he was antiquated, one of the classics "of an Age that heard of none" (1:103, 149).

Some writers questioned whether language was capable of genuine clarity. Three substantial chapters of book 3 of the *Essay concerning Human Understanding* are devoted to the "Imperfections of Words," which by their "very nature" are often "doubtful and uncertain in their significations" (2:104). Locke's warnings were echoed through the eighteenth century, not only by poets and novelists but also by some of the grammarians and philosophers who were most publicly committed to the value of precise thinking (Flanders, 91). The well-worn and indeed venerable comic figure of the scholar/pedant/dunce was revived and brought to vigorous, dynamic life by Swift, Pope, Arbuthnot, and the Scriblerians: "Words alone" are his province; "on Words is still our whole debate" (*Dunciad*, 4:149, 219), implying that knowledge of words alone is either false or inadequate knowledge. The faculty of Swift's Grand Academy of Lagado experiments with a word machine for the mechanical production of "a complete body of all arts and sciences" pieced together from "broken sentences" (Swift, 131, 148, 150); that is, the most erudite students of language may make fools of themselves in their attempts to employ it as an instrument for expressing truth. Johnson complains at length and with startling clarity of "words too plain to admit a definition" and of words "too subtile and evanescent to be fixed in a paraphrase," of verbs that the lexicographer tries in vain to catch "on the brink of utter inanity," and of terms "which I cannot explain, because I do not understand them" (*Works*, 5:34–35). Campbell devotes a section of *The Philosophy of Rhetoric* to explaining the "phenomena, that a man of sense should sometimes write nonsense and not know it, and that a man of sense should sometimes read nonsense, and imagine he understands it" (265).

As a whole, however, the age retained a robust confidence in language as a medium for expressing ideas, a medium that could be refined, corrected, and improved by men of learning. Dryden furnishes the most striking example of a writer setting out to prune colloquial, disorderly, and old-fashioned locutions from his own works, substituting more elegant locutions, more precise and modern. The *Essay of Dramatic Poesy*, despite its date—it was published in 1668, fifty-four years before *Moll Flanders*—reads more like educated twentieth-century English than *Moll Flanders* does:

> In the mean time I must desire you to take notice, that the greatest man of the last age (*Ben Johnson*) was willing to give place to them in all things: He was not only a professed Imitator of *Horace*, but a learned Plagiary of all the others; you track him every where in their Snow: If *Horace, Lucan, Petronious Arbiter, Seneca*, and *Juvenal* had their own from him, there are few serious thoughts which are new in him; you will pardon me therefore if I presume he lov'd their fashion when he wore their cloaths.[9]

This paragraph is one of Dryden's best-known, most beautifully turned judgments. By its side, the prosings of the old hack Moll seem shapeless and dowdy.

How does the *Essay* fare when we subject it to the same scrutiny as *Moll*? Although there are a certain number of colloquial, disorderly, and old-fashioned locutions in the *Essay*, its overall texture is very different from that of Defoe's novel. Only two homely shopkeepers' idioms occur in the first one-third of the *Essay*, and only one colloquial asseveration:

> they scap'd not so good cheap. (24)
>
> I have seen them reading in the midst of Change-time; nay so vehement they were at it, that they lost their bargain by the Candles ends. (12)

Topicalizations with *as to*, *as for*, and *for* occur several times in the 8,200 words I examined, but they do not assert themselves in the lunging manner associated with lower-class speech. There is nothing in *An Essay of Dramatic Poesy* that corresponds to "out of the World by the Steps and the String" or "Mother Midnight" or "*viz.*," "as they say," "What!" "Why," "Carry it again? Carry it again!" or the celebrated looseness of but-and-which chains in *Moll Flanders*. It is reasonable to conclude that *An Essay of Dramatic Poesy*, though dialogue, is not colloquial at all in the sense that *Moll Flanders* is.

I found some sloppiness in the *Essay*, including one clear failure to write parallel constructions:

> They can produce nothing so courtly writ, or which expresses so much the Conversation of a Gentleman. (1)

In several instances, Dryden does not keep his pronouns straight:

> he had a rude Notion of it; indeed rather a Description than a Definition: but which serv'd to guide him. (14)

> things . . . whose wit depended on some custom . . . or perhaps on some Criticism in their language, which being so long dead, . . . 'tis not possible they should make us know it perfectly. (21–22)

Strictly speaking, this is a dangling participle:

> Having then so much care to excel in one kind, very little is to be pardon'd them. (2)

Redundancy does not figure to any appreciable extent in the *Essay*. And compared to the first 8,200 words of *Moll Flanders*, the first 8,200 words of the *Essay* are noticeably free of solecism, vague and slapdash wording. The first 2,000 words of the *Essay*, which Dryden may be supposed to have taken most pains with, do not make any mistakes of this kind at all.

The language of the *Essay* reveals its date in a number of unobtrusive ways. Though it eschews double negatives, puts auxiliaries to modern uses, and altogether abandons a-verbing constructions, heavy datives, and the 'had-X-done-this, Y-had-done-that' idiom, its conjunctions are not entirely modern:

> except we have the confidence to say. (17)
>
> the Characters are indeed the Imitations of Nature, but so narrow as if they had imitated only an Eye. (25)

One old-fashioned intensifier, "exceeding great," occurs in the first third of the *Essay* (9), and once Dryden uses *that* to gather in and point to earlier references:

> a Scene or two of tenderness, and that where you would least expect it. (31)

Since we find this last construction in Fielding and Richardson (especially in Clarissa's will), Defoe's fondness for it will count as a cumbersome quirk, not as a blunder.

Dryden's handling of negatives and quantifiers belongs more often to the mid-seventeenth century than to the mid-eighteenth:

> no Poet but may sometimes use. (29)
>
> no man but must have yielded. (31)
>
> I can never see one of those Plays which are not writtten, but it encreases my admiration of the Ancients. (20)
>
> We neither find it in *Aristotle, Horace,* or any who have written of it. (36)
>
> Unity of Place . . . was never any of their Rules. (26)
>
> in a less compass. (27)
>
> the *Medea* is none of his. (31)
>
> the Ancients meant no other by it than what the Logicians do. (19)
>
> to omit many other drawn from the Precepts and Practice of the Ancients. (20)

Almost every history of English takes note of the evolution of negatives with auxiliaries during the seventeenth century—"not" in Shakespeare commonly follows the verb: "I care not who knows" (*Twelfth Night*, III, iv, 272) and "guilt shows not itself" (*Twelfth*

Night, III, ii, 147), where we would say, 'I do not care', 'guilt does not show'. Here Dryden is less modern than Defoe:

> such as understood not theirs. (17)
>
> you behold him not. (18)
>
> we draw not. (22; additional examples 17, 18, 22)

Despite this collection of antique traits and features, the texture of Dryden's prose is not only shiny-new, compared to Defoe's, but also *intended* to be shiny-new, a fact that revisions for the second edition of 1684 make clear. The extent of Defoe's awareness of the archaisms he puts in Moll's mouth, I should not care to decide; but Dryden's awareness of the value of modernity and elegance in the *Essay* is unquestionable. Most of the fifty to sixty changes in our sample speak directly to this issue. Dryden replaces shopkeepers' lingo with repectable lexical items (a "wench" becomes a "mistress" [25], "garboyles" become "disorders" [26]), and he strikes out old-fashioned idioms, substituting modern ones:

1668	1684
guess of Menander's Excellency	guess at. (20)
the Tragedies . . . are to be had	are in our hands. (20)
borrows of	borrows from. (22)
managing of them	management of them. (27)
a hundred or two of Verses	a hundred or more Verses. (24)
or who lately were so	or who lately were. (14)

He adjusts his pronouns and prepositions:

one that is so much a well-wisher	one who is so much. (10)
Poets, which	Poets, who. (17, 19)
many things . . . whose wit	the wit of which. (20)
whom all the Story is built upon	on whom the Story is built. (25)

44

At least one change supplies end-focus where there was none in 1668:

I will produce Father "Ben" to you	I will produce before you Father "Ben." (21)

And in two cases Dryden corrects vague or ambiguous pronoun reference:

told "Eugenius" he approv'd his Propositions, and, if he pleased, he would limit . . .	told "Eugenius" that if he pleased, he would limit. (13)
they set the Audience . . . where the Race is to be concluded: and, saving them the tedious expectation of seeing the Poet . . . , you behold him not	they set the Audience . . . where the Race is to be concluded: and, saving them the tedious expectation of seeing the Poet . . . , they suffer you not to behold him. (18)

The evidence of Dryden's revisions, then, justifies a school-teacherly approach to Defoe's prose and prompts us to think of grammatical-linguistic standards of the age itself as a context within which Moll Flanders's idiosyncrasies are all the more noticeable and significant.

III. Prescriptive Grammars

If Dryden and Pope corrected their own writings so scrupulously, if Swift published a formal *Proposal for Correcting . . . the English Tongue* in 1712, if Johnson's *Dictionary* (1755) was written partly to increase the "purity" and "propriety," to diminish the "barbarity" and "capriciousness" of the English language, if, in other words, major authors of the period were engaged in eradicating solecisms, archaisms, and colloquialisms, each in his own way, what were grammarians of the time up to? How did their activities accelerate or obstruct the development of prescriptivism in eighteenth-century England? "Were we as industrious in improving and cultivating our Language, as the *Greeks* and *Romans* were, we might equal if not exceed them," wrote A. Lane in 1700, in the preface to an early English grammar for schoolchildren. It seems reasonable to expect that grammatical handbooks joined the battle against colloquialism, incorrectness, and archaism, and may thereby be cited to clarify criteria for lower-class English.

In fact, eighteenth-century grammarians are eager recruits in the war against vulgar language, eager but, up to 1760 or 1770, inept. In fact, before the last third of the century, very few English writers of any ilk produced texts that are free of colloquialisms, solecisms, and archaisms, no matter how devoted in theory they were to correctness and perspicuity. Before Johnson (1755), Lowth (1762), Kames (1762), and Campbell (1776), most grammarians are guilty of colloquialism, solecisms, and archaisms in the very work they have written (in part) to attack these faults.

It took time to translate neoclassicist and prescriptive ideals into practical rules that apprentice authors could apply to their own writing. Before about 1760, English grammars and grammatical handbooks give relatively few specific directions for attaining correctness and perspicuity. After Lowth (forty-five editions, 1762–1800; see Alston, 1965), and his popularizer, John Ash (forty-one editions, 1763–1800), and his emulators and rivals such as John Burn (ten editions, 1766–1810), James Buchanan (seven editions, 1767–92), and Daniel Fenning (nine editions, 1771–1800), all English grammars and handbooks and the equally influential public lectures of such distinguished thinkers as George Campbell and Hugh Blair gave voluminous specific instructions for correcting and clarifying one's prose.

The next few pages, then, present evidence from the grammarians that will prohibit us from employing our model of lower-class English on texts published before 1760 or 1770. In spite of widespread anxiety about the unruliness of the language, English grammars of the first half of the eighteenth century were not very prescriptive; that is, they did not formulate rules for correctness or censure specific errors. The second half of the century saw a big increase in the number of grammars (and other publications interested in grammar) and repeated attempts to prescribe good English and to condemn particular errors, and therefore a new order of sensitivity to just those linguistic traits that differentiate the language of the educated upper classes from the language of the illiterate mob.

R. C. Alston lists only about 106 publications on grammar from 1700 to 1750, but almost 400 between 1751 and 1800 (this includes different editions and reissues of the same titles). Ian Michael lists 38 separate titles, including dictionaries, spelling-books, philosophical lectures, and such volumes as *The Lady's Polite Secretary*, for 1700–1750, and 199 separate titles for 1751–1800. The ratios of four to one and five to one respectively can be taken as evidence that in spite of Swift and Pope it was not till the 1750s that the general public began to be caught up in grammatical issues.

Why the 1750s? The number of grammars tripled in that decade. According to Michael, there were four grammatical publications in the 1720s, thirteen in the 1730s, and seven in the 1740s, versus twenty-three in the 1750s, thirty-three in the 1760s, and fifty-two in the 1770s. Also, it is in the 1750s and early 1760s that heavy artillery of the learned world begins to rumble on topics related to correctness. In the first half of the eighteenth century, the most celebrated name on the list of authors of English grammars is surely that of John Wesley, who did not offer his *Short English Grammar* (1748) as a major contribution; it is a simple text for schoolchildren. All the other names before Johnson (1755) are minor figures at best (A. Lane, James Greenwood, John Collyer, John Kirkby, James Corbet, etc.). Samuel Johnson's *Dictionary* of 1755 is epoch-making in this as in other respects, and he was followed by Joseph Priestley (1761), by Henry Home, Lord Kames (1762), by Bishop Robert Lowth (1762), by the lectures of Hugh Blair (from 1759 on), as well as by the discourses George Campbell prepared for a philosophical club in Aberdeen during the 1760s, later published as *The Philosophy of Rhetoric* (1776).

All six of these men were formidable scholars who have earned secure places in the history of ideas, independent of what they published on correctness in English grammar. Johnson was at once in the first rank of poets, essayists, moralists, lexicographers, and literary critics. Priestley, an incisive liberal thinker on theology, education, and politics, was the ablest experimental chemist of his time, co-discoverer of oxygen. Kames, Blair, and Campbell were major literary-philosophical figures in the Scottish Renaissance. The first had won reputation by his *Essay on the Principles of Morality and Natural Religion* (1751) and his *Introduction to the Art of Thinking* (1761); the other two lectured and taught actively for years in principal Scots universities before their major works were published.

47

Lowth, formerly the Professor of Poetry at Oxford, had published his lectures on Hebrew poetry in 1752 and was appointed Bishop of London in 1777.

A careful sampling of English grammars before 1751, moreover, does not uncover very much in the way of prescriptivism. Lane, in a *A Key to the Art of Letters* (1700), for example, announces on the title page his desire "to enable both Foreiners [*sic*], and the *English* youth of either Sex, to speak and write the *English* Tongue well and learnedly, according to the exactest Rules of *Grammar*," but the first mention of any particular offense against correctness or taste in its 122 small pages occurs on page 36, in passing, as part of a discussion of miscellaneous adjectives: "Many a man, *is a barbarism, first used among the vulgar for many men.*" What makes this prescriptive, not merely descriptive, is its emphasis on social class ("*vulgar*") and civilizedness ("*barbarism*"), and it is worth noting that the feature Lane censures is in fact an archaism as well, perfectly correct in Elizabethan English only one hundred years earlier. Most of Lane's book is occupied with telling us what English grammar is, without overt mention of how it should be. Thus, Lane a few pages later identifies the subjunctive as a verb "joined to another verb, by the final conjunction, *that*, as, *I read* that *I may learn*," but he does not lecture or admonish the reader, as do later grammarians, on the ignorance, vulgarity, or incorrectness of failing to use the subjunctive in its proper place. Lane disposes of irregular verbs—the grounds, in later grammars, of many a stricture, many a rule—in one short question and answer:

> Q. *Is not the Pretertense sometimes irregularly formed?*
> A. The Preter tense is often irregularly formed, as from *see, saw*; from *run, ran*; from *break, broke*; with many more, which use will teach. (48)

Lane's book is a school text, designed for young people who were not planning to learn Latin or go to a university, so it is relatively short, and it makes no pretensions to going beyond the essentials. This seems to be true of all eighteenth-century English grammars before James Harris's *Hermes* of 1751, which is more philosophical than prescriptive. Thus, Thomas Dilworth's *New Guide to the English Tongue* (1740), of which Alston counts more than a hundred editions from 1740 to 1800, and of which "at least a million copies were printed" during this period, is largely a spelling-book but includes a short grammar on pages 85–126, "to enable such as are intended to rise no higher, to write their *Mother-Tongue* intelligibly, and according to the *Rules of Grammar*" (viii), so that they will read *The Spectator* and *Tatler*, not "*Grubstreet Papers, idle Pamphlets, lewd Plays, filthy Songs*" (ix). Dilworth's volume contains no prescriptivism at all, unless one counts the example of "unintelligible" English he supplies in his two-page chapter on syntax: "Beaten not are Boys good" (121). Ann Fisher, whose *New Grammar* of 1750—half a century after Lane—ran to at least thirty-five editions before 1800, was the wife of a Newcastle printer, a fact that shows up in some of her rules for pronunciation: *k* before *n* "always changes its Sound for that of *h*" (24); "the proper Sound of *gh* is out of the Throat" (22). But I count only five places in a 158-page book where she allows herself to be prescriptive: in her mention of double superlatives (83), on the prefix *a-* ("very improperly" used for *in*, e.g., *a-bed* [100]), on *which* for people, as in the Lord's Prayer (121), on double negatives ("Solecisms" [120]), and on inversions of the "natural" word order ("the clearest and best Writers in *Prose* have the fewest *Transpositions*" [123]). All five are either perfectly normal or more frequent in Elizabethan English.[10]

Not only are English grammarians from 1700 to 1750 relatively innocent of prescriptivism; they are also in need of it. In one degree or another, all of them commit what Lowth in 1762 would call solecisms, and all employ some archaic syntax. Lowth (122–24) rules that "Every Verb hath its Nominative Case," that is, a subject, and quotes *Gulliver's Travels:* "A man, whose inclinations led him to be corrupt, and had great abilities"—the second verb here, "had," lacks an explicit subject (such as "who"). Brightland and Gildon (*A Grammar of the English Tongue*, 1711) ask "if there be any Character . . . that does not express a sound entirely simple, but a Sound compos'd and compounded of two or more, and is resoluble into as many . . ." (iii). The same error—really, lack of explicitness and therefore lack of perfect clarity—crops up twice in one sentence by Dilworth (1740): "It serves to include one Sentence in another, without confounding the Sense of either; and yet is necessary for the Explanation thereof: And should be read with a lower Tone" (93).

Additional examples could be supplied by the hundreds. Lowth remonstrates against employing adjectives as adverbs (125). *The En-*

glish Accidence (1733) avers that those who fail to study grammar "can neither spell nor point [punctuate]" though "they may pronounce and speak proper enough by practice" (iv). Lowth has severe things to say on the logic of sequence of tenses. The preface to Brightland and Gildon's *Grammar of the English Tongue* states that a certain person "found himself just where he set out" (A4v). "If our parents are careful . . . and did instill *religion* and *morality* in us . . . ," says *The English Accidence*. Lowth makes agreement of subject and verb, adjective and noun, one of his cardinal principles. Thomas Dyche, in *A Guide to the English Tongue* (1707), affirms that "if the Consonant *j* be always tail'd . . . , there needs no further Rules" to distinguish it from *i* (110).

Faulty pronoun reference, nonparallel constructions, and misplaced modifiers all play a prominent role in chapter 18 of Lord Kames's *Elements of Criticism* (seven editions, 1762–1800, plus one each in Dublin, Basel, and Boston). Following tradition, Kames lists perspicuity as a primary virtue of prose. What is not traditional about this chapter, what is new in English criticism, is a detailed analysis of "offenses against perspicuity" in relatively recent and respected English authors, especially Swift, Bolingbroke, Addison, and Steele. On a single page (259) Kames quotes *Spectators* 265 and 530, Swift's *Abolishing Christianity* and *Dissertation upon Parties*, Dryden's *Aeneid*, *Guardian* 139, and *Coriolanus, Julius Caesar*, and the *Merchant of Venice*, correcting such infelicities as "had he not found an opportunity to escape out of his hands, and *fled* into the deserts" (*Guardian* 139; italics added by Kames).

If Kames or Lowth had read early English grammars with the same care as they read Swift, many of the same faults would have appeared, plus a good deal of writing more slovenly than anything in Swift. James Greenwood begins his *Practical English Grammar* of 1711, "Man, tho' he has great Variety of thoughts, and such from which others, as well as himself, might receive Profit and Delight; yet they are all within his own Breast . . ." (33). He discusses the parts of speech, "all which Words you shall be plainly taught how to know one from the other" (40). "No *English* Word ends in *I* but has always an *E* after it" (240). Ann Fisher (1750) defines orthography as "The Art of true Spelling, which teaches to write every Word with proper Letters: But as concern'd in Pronunciation, it shews how to give the due Sound of them" (2). "*What is the second Irregularity* in verbs," she asks, and gives as answer, "Some Words, whose

present Time end in *d* or *t*, the *past Time* is the same as the *present*"
(90). As an example of proper agreement between pronoun and
antecedent, Hugh Jones has, "I heard the Boy, which had learnt his
Lesson, and commended him" (39). William Loughton tells us that
"Comparison of Qualities serves to distinguish the different degrees of qualities of the like kind, and whereby we affirm of things
that one is of such a quality, another more such, and a third most
such" (58).

Archaisms are if anything more commonplace in early eighteenth-century English grammars than are solecisms. We find the
Elizabethan verb *to be*, descended from Anglo-Saxon *beon* (not
wesan), in John Entick in 1728: "It teacheth the artificial Disposition
of Words, which be not naturally ranged together, yet are intelli-
gable [*sic*]" (27). Old-fashioned past participles linger on in most
discussions of irregular verbs, *shotten* for *shoot*, *spitten* for *spit*, *slid-
den* for *slide* (these three from Kirkby, 1746). Early Modern English
had more impersonals than Present-day English does, for example,
"there belong to a *Pronoun, Number, Case, Gender*," and more
datives, for example, "*Conjugate me the Verb Active* Educate" (these
two from Dilworth, 102, 107). "Would you avoid" misspelling homonyms, says Samuel Saxon in 1737, "you must be very careful in your
Observations thereupon" (27).

I do not mean to overstate my case. One or two of the early
grammars may run on for many pages without solecisms and archaisms (e.g., Kirkby, 1746, and Gough, 1754). Elsewhere, what I call
archaisms are little more than old-fashioned turns of speech, such
as would not have seemed out of place outside the cultural mainstream even after 1760. For the sake of clarity, I have not done justice
here to the fact that natural languages change slowly (except in
catastrophic circumstances), irregularly, and often beyond the consciousness of the most self-conscious writers. It is quite easy to find
archaisms in Johnson, though not so easy in Lowth. The two Scots,
Kames and Campbell, are still more scrupulous to avoid obsolete
words and diction. To complicate things further, Johnson is perhaps the second major English writer, after Swift, to adopt archaic
locutions into his own personal style—I am thinking of extended
inversions, as in the *Preface* to his edition of Shakespeare of 1765,
"To works, however, of which the excellence is not absolute and de-
finitive, but gradual and comparative: to works not [X] but [Y], no
other test can be applied than . . ." (135). I wonder whether even

Johnson was aware that Elizabethan word order was more flexible than eighteenth-century word order, or that such inversions were a mildly archaic feature of his prose. What strikes us as an archaism in Fielding, his persistent use of *hath* as the third person singular of *to have*, was probably intended as a way of differentiating clearly among verb forms; Lowth does the same.

When we turn to the major prescriptivists of 1755–76, however, we can hardly fail to see a difference between them and their predecessors. Before 1750, almost all grammars are short, puerile, slovenly, and old-fashioned. Principal grammatical publications after 1750 are long, learned, precise, and modern. The last step in my argument, then, is to assess the force and quality of prescriptivism in Johnson, Lowth, Kames, and Campbell, taking these four as both representative and exemplary of the new linguistic self-consciousness of the second half of the eighteenth century.

Though the Dodsleys—most literary of booksellers—published *A Short Introduction to English Grammar* anonymously in 1762, this handsome volume was known to have been written by a former Oxford professor, author of *De sacra poesi Hebraeium* (1753), Robert Lowth (1710–87), later Bishop of London. It is an elegant book, even in facsimile: spacious margins, large, generously leaded type, the prose style of a gentleman and a scholar. The physical contrast between this English grammar and its numerous, poorly printed antecedents is unmistakable. The "principal Design" of any grammar, writes Lowth, is "to teach us to express ourselves with propriety in that Language," which is a perfectly conventional goal; but Lowth goes on, "and to be able to judge of every phrase and form of construction, whether it be right or not." (x) This is new.

To advance his readers' ability to judge correctness, Lowth refers them to his notes:

> But perhaps the Notes subjoined to the following pages will furnish a more convincing argument, than any thing that can be said here, both of the truth of the charge of inaccuracy brought against our Language as it subsists in practice, and of the necessity of investigating the Principles of it, and studying it Grammatically, if we would attain to a due degree of skill in it. It is with reason expected of every person of a liberal education, and much more is it indispensibly required of every one who undertakes to inform or entertain the public, that he should be able to ex-

press himself with propriety and accuracy. It will evidently appear from these Notes, that our best Authors for want of some rudiments of this kind have sometimes fallen into mistakes, and been guilty of palpable errors in point of Grammar. (viii–ix)

As if to announce his willingness to take on all comers, Lowth, in the first of these notes (16–18), engages to correct three passages from the King James Bible in their use of definite and indefinite articles. Bishop Atterbury receives a slap on the wrist in the second note, and an expression in the Bible is described as "obsolete, or at least vulgar," that is, archaic, low-class, or colloquial. The next note identifies *eyen* and *shoen* as out of date (23). Addison, Matthew Prior, Milton, Dryden, Addison again (twice more), Bolingbroke (twice), and Pope (thrice) are quoted and rewritten in notes scattered among pages 26–52. Archbishop John Tillotson, Swift, Atterbury, the Earl of Clarendon, Swift again, the third Earl of Shaftesbury, and Addison yet again are displayed in violation of one rule or another at the bottom of pages 63–99. In the last four pages of the *Grammar*, Lowth quotes six faulty locutions from Swift, six from Clarendon, two from Pope, and one each from Addison, Atterbury, Dryden, Conyers Middleton, Sir William Temple, and Tillotson, that is, from a major historian, a classicist/biographer, two bishops, two of the foremost essayists of the time, a poet laureate, the greatest poet, and the supreme prose satirist of the eighteenth century. Again, the contrast between Lowth and his predecessors, who do not refer to authors of this rank except to flatter them, is glaring.

What are the qualities of Lowth's prescriptivism? It is learned but not pedantic. Lowth quotes from the best, most scholarly of his predecessors: John Wilkins, George Hickes, Johnson, Harris; he refers to the voluminous Ward, and makes easy allusion to grammatical practice in Anglo-Saxon, German, French, Latin, and Greek. Remove the footnotes, however, and one is left with exactly what is promised by the title, except that this is a fairly thorough "introduction," not just an outline or sketch.

Lowth's prescriptivism is also forceful. He is capable of strong language. Confusion between the preterite and the past participle of verbs, where different forms exist, he terms "a very great Corruption" (85), and *you was* (which we find throughout Boswell's journals) he calls an "enormous Solecism" (48).

> We should be immediately shocked at *I have knew, I have
> saw, I have gave,* &c: but our ears are grown familiar with *I
> have wrote, I have drank, I have bore,* &c. which are alto-
> gether as barbarous. (90)

Unequivocally judgmental expressions in Lowth, however, are not
incompatible with a controlled, cultivated stance; he is not a ranter
like Bentley. "The impropriety of the Phrases distinguished [above]
by Italic Characters is evident," he remarks following a long quotation from Tillotson's sermons.

More centrally, Lowth's prescriptivism is classical but British;
that is, it aims at clarity and order, strives to preserve distinctions
and be precise, but is not perfectly consistent; it respects the English language and is willing to accept ambiguity, or even a version
of contextualism, where recommended by common sense and good
taste. Clarity is Lowth's first goal, a fact that may partially account
for the astonishing durability of some of his rules. Most of what
is taught as correct English in twentieth-century American grade
schools, if anything at all is, derives from Lowth, or, slightly
amended, from Lowth's followers (e.g. Lindley Murray, whose *English Grammar* [1795] ran to hundreds of editions in Britain and
America).

> In general, the omission of the Relative [e.g., "the man I
> love"] seems to be too much indulged in the familiar style;
> it is ungraceful in the serious; and of whatever kind the
> style be, it is apt to be attended with obscurity and ambigu-
> ity. (137)

The subjunctive, from Lowth's point of view, is worth preserving
and regularizing because it enables English-speakers to make a distinction between "Hypothetical, Conditional, Concessive, and Ex-
ceptive" statements, and others (140−41).

On the other hand, Lowth rejects the traditional view that English is inferior to Latin and Greek because it has fewer inflections.
One of his first notes argues that the English system of articles is
more excellent than the Greek because it more "precisely determine[s] the extent of signification of Common [vs. proper] Names"
(18). The "simplicity" of English, in which it excels even Hebrew, is
not a fault of the language, though it has given rise to that neglect

of grammar of which Swift and so many others have complained (v–vi). Lowth acknowledges the poetical beauties of the Elizabethan pronoun system at the same time as he criticizes inconsistency in the pronouns of a verse from the 1611 translation of Ecclesiastes (35). He is willing to accept ambiguity in the English auxiliaries: "*should* in the Imperfect Times, is used to express the Present, as well as the Past . . .; so that in this Mode the precise Time of the Verb is very much determined by the nature and drift of the Sentence" (55).

Not that Lowth's book in 1762 is the sudden incarnation of the whole grammatical truth. He is capable of fussiness, obtuseness, and misunderstanding. For example, he is unreasonably particular over getting the "right" preposition with certain verbs, and scolds Swift for an "impropriety" in writing: "You have bestowed your favours *to* the most deserving persons" rather than *upon* the most deserving persons (129). Seduced by a theory that seems to offer to explain things neatly—he is not the only grammarian to have been so seduced—he proposes that all infinitives be considered as "substantives" and all participles as adjectives, and then in a note blames Swift for using an infinitive nonsubstantively (111). Time has ratified most of his rules because they make sense and conduce to clarity—most but not all; some seem laughable today, and one or two are mere curiosities.[11]

For our purposes, what is most important about Lowth is that his prescriptivism, in addition to its forcefulness, elegance, and authority, is directed almost entirely against solecisms and archaisms in written texts. If Lowth's rules are listed and classified, almost half proscribe locutions that were perfectly acceptable in Shakespeare's time: possessives such as *Bob his book* (26), *whose* used indiscriminately for people and things (38, 133–34), double superlatives (42), *which* as a conjunction (124), etc. (Colloquialisms figure less prominently, perhaps because Lowth takes it for granted that down-at-the-heels locutions do not belong in written texts, but he does outlaw *never so* as an intensifier [147].) Many of the archaisms Lowth attacks are also illogical, inconsistent, or unclear; that is, they are solecisms. For example, a proper sequence of tenses requires that some past events be marked as having happened earlier than other past events, when that is true and pertinent, but Elizabethan English was not so choosy (118).

Kames's *Elements of Criticism*, which also appeared in 1762, neatly complements Lowth's emphasis on grammar by its concern with discourse. The subject of Kames's book is aesthetics; he does not get around to being prescriptive until chapter 18, "Beauty of Language," but once he has established "perspicuity" as a primary beauty of language (255), twenty-seven close-printed pages go by before he finishes with "want of perspicuity" in its various aspects. Under his two main headings, "wrong choice of words" and "wrong arrangement" of words, he talks about a variety of defects, including elegant variation (257) and merely verbal antitheses (259), but his most telling criticisms against recent English authors are largely related to the principles of parallel construction and "juxtaposition." Swift, Bolingbroke, Shaftesbury, Hume, Addison, Robert Hook, Swift again, and Addison again are arraigned for lack of parallel construction, infelicities like the following in the *Proposal for Correcting the English Tongue*: "I have observed of late, the style of some great *ministers* very much to exceed that of any other *productions*" (261, Kames's italics). "Juxtaposition is our chief resource" in English for showing near relationship, says Kames (267), which is why inaccurate pronoun reference and misplacement of modifiers may so grievously disfigure the works even of such celebrated authors as (once more) Swift, Addison, Bolingbroke, and Shaftesbury, sixteen examples from whom are corrected in four pages.

Samuel Johnson made himself felt as a champion of prescriptivism earlier than Lowth or Kames, in the great *Dictionary* of 1755 and its *Plan* of 1747; but the quality of his prescriptivism is ambivalent, partly because he was not as explicit or detailed in his rejection of solecisms as the two younger authors were, partly because there were some archaisms that he favored, not condemned, and partly because he seems to have understood more clearly than his contemporaries the organic nature of language. European lexicographical traditions of the seventeenth and eighteenth centuries made it almost impossible that a big, serious dictionary could be anything but prescriptive. People had been lamenting the lack of an authoritative English dictionary, to fix the language and establish standards of correctness, since Richard Mulcaster in the 1580s (see Sledd and Kolb), and both the *Plan* and the "Preface" of Johnson's *Dictionary* recognize a need for regularity, "purity," modernity, and correctness in English. The *Plan* mentions at least two kinds of "barbarities" and quotes two of the same passages as Lowth does, where Addison writes *lesser* and Dryden writes *worser*. The "licentiousness," "capriciousness," "perplexity," and "wild exuberance" of the English language is a first premise for Johnson's labors.

The *Dictionary* itself, however, does not dispense many rules. Among its prefatory materials is a short grammar, written to accompany an even more perfunctory history of the language, but Johnson's heart was not in either one. He runs through the alphabet and the parts of speech without much system or detail, pausing briefly to observe that even "good writers" blunder in their use of comparatives, that *you* is replacing *thou* and *ye*, as *hath* is giving way to the more "corrupted" *has*, and that pleonastic *do* "is considered as a vitious mode of speech." Additional rules or judgments as to grammatical correctness in Johnson's "Grammar" can be counted on the fingers of one hand.[12]

Once afloat among the 41,000 entries of the main *Dictionary*, readers will not find it easy to say exactly how prescriptive Johnson desires to be. On the one hand, he identifies some 800 words, according to one count (Allen), as "low," "barbarous," or vulgar, which is more than any earlier dictionary had done. But 800 is not a large number among 41,000, considering the fact that the supplement alone of Eric Partridge's *Dictionary of Slang and Unconventional English* (1970) runs to more than 100,000 entries. On the one hand, where Johnson did express his opinions, they were often noticed and quoted, as when Lowth cites Johnson as his authority for stigmatizing *never so* as a solecism. On the other, the same scholar who counted 800 censured words in the *Dictionary* also followed up the subsequent history of these 800 words and could not find that Johnson's disapproval had had any noticeable effect on their vitality or currency. The *Dictionary* in general is hostile to colloquialisms, without doubt, as the preface makes clear when acknowledging that language change is inevitable:

> Illiterate writers will, at one time or other, by publick infatuation, rise into renown, who, not knowing the original import of words, will use them with colloquial licentiousness, confound distinction, and forget propriety. (*Works*, 5:48)

In Johnson's mind, words "of which no original can be found" are cant words, "low terms, the spawn of folly or affectation" (*Works*, 5:11); and often such words are colloquial. Thus, he admits *fun* in the *Dictionary*, because it is common, but he brands it "A low cant word," of uncertain etymology. *Funny* he does not list at all, even in the revised edition of 1784, though it was in active use and in print by 1762 at least.

On archaisms, Johnson is ambivalent. Having denominated early seventeenth-century English from 1590 to 1660 as "*the wells of English undefiled*" on which his word-lists will be based, he then labels a substantial number of words that were actively in use during this period as obsolete. I do not know how to reconcile this contradiction without some other criterion for lexical validity than currency between 1590 and 1660, that is, some standards for deciding in 1755 which of all the words in use since 1590 were current and which were out of date. I sense in Johnson some disposition to favor those archaisms that seemed to him worthy of preservation. *Actually*, 'that which comprises action', was not current in the eighteenth century (last *OED* citation: 1647), but he does not mark the word as obsolete. *Addice* is listed as a word "for which we corruptly speak and write *ads*." Some of the archaisms proscribed in Lowth have also been proscribed in Johnson, but most have not: he allows *whose* to refer to inanimates, with Shakespeare and Prior as examples; *exceeding* used as an adverb "is not analogical, but has been long admitted and established" (however, *right*, *mighty*, and *wondrous* used as adverbs are branded as obsolete, low, and barbarous respectively); he accepts *that* for *that which*; and despite the rule laid down in his "Grammar" (which was written years after most of the entries for the *Dictionary* proper), he seems more relaxed than Lowth in recognizing alternative preterites and past participles for strong verbs, for example, *writ* or *wrote* as preterite, *written*, *writ*, or *wrote* as past participles, *began* or *begun* as preterites. By looking up Early Modern English subordinate conjunctions in Johnson's *Dictionary*, one can uncover a number of words current in Shakespeare's time that Johnson omits (*bithat*, *cause*, *forcause*, *forbecause*, *forthan*, *syn*), a number that he includes without marking them as obsolete (*for that*, *forwhy*, *that* meaning 'because', *but* meaning 'if', *and* meaning 'if'), and a number that he indicates are "obsolete" or "not in use" (*sith*, *and if*, *without* meaning 'unless', *whiles*, *whereas* meaning 'where') (see McIntosh, "Evolution").

We might expect Johnson to go on record as an enemy of lower-class linguistic features in his edition of Shakespeare, published in 1765. The notes to individual plays were intended to "disentangle" any obscurities arising from vulgar, colloquial, or archaic language, and to observe "faults and beauties" in particular passages. In the 1756 *Proposals* for an edition, he alludes to his own uniquely extensive acquaintance with "obsolete or peculiar diction," acquired while "beating the track of the alphabet with sluggish resolution" for the *Dictionary*. The same document observes that the difficulty of some passages in Shakespeare derives from dependency on "the common, colloquial language" (*Shakespeare*, 53, 56–57). But Johnson's notes to individual plays do not answer these expectations; or, rather, Johnson as editor of Shakespeare is prescriptive only in passing.

Some words are said to be "harsh," some passages "confused," and a few expressions are identified as archaic or colloquial.[13] What calls up the critic in Johnson, however, is more frequently the license of Shakespeare's editors than of Shakespeare himself. He passes up the chance to correct *lesser* in *Midsummer Night's Dream*, II, ii, to explain *for that* as a causal conjunction (*MND*, II, i), and to censure *never so* (*As You Like It*, III, ii, 164). He prefers "the old and proper word" *momentany* to the newer word, *momentary* (*MND*, I, i).

The picture that emerges from these different perspectives is of tremendous but perhaps capricious authority. Known for the judiciousness and accuracy of his writing in the 1740s, heralded by Chesterfield (and the booksellers) as the long-awaited lawgiver to our "barbarous" language, self-proclaimed in the *Plan* and the "Preface" as an arbiter of good usage, Johnson is nevertheless unpredictable in general and predisposed on occasion to favor words and phrases that are now considered native to Early Modern English, the English of Shakespeare's time. Extremely respectful allusions to Johnson by Lowth, Campbell, and other prescriptivists, however, confirm his reputation as a champion of correctness.

The Philosophy of Rhetoric by George Campbell, published in 1776, not only rectifies some of the inconsistencies in Johnson and expatiates on rules in Lowth and Kames but also explains, substantiates, and exemplifies the principles of prescriptivism in general. It is a formidable book, 415 close-packed pages, many passages of it brilliantly written. Most of the last 300 of its pages are devoted to the explication of standards of "precision," "perspicuity" (152), "purity," "simplicity," "elegance," and "harmony" (168) that are extremely unfriendly to just those usages that our hypothesis ascribes to lower-class speakers.

COMMON AND COURTLY LANGUAGE

I do not wish to give the impression any more of Campbell than of Lowth that in this author the English language had at last found a philosopher-king whose book encapsulates "true," modern standards of grammatical correctness. S. A. Leonard has demonstrated, exhaustively, the degree to which prescriptivists disagreed with each other and derided each other's positions. What I argue, rather, is that in the third quarter of the eighteenth century, following the authoritative leadership of Johnson, Lowth, Kames, Campbell, and others, no writer could pretend to elegance or educated excellence in prose who permitted large numbers of solecisms, archaisms, and colloquialisms in his or her published works, except in burlesque and low comedy. Low-class language for the first time was defined, identified, and its qualities enumerated. The doctrine that certain kinds of language were not suitable for high seriousness is as old as rhetoric itself, but self-consciousness about a large number of specific features of low English was not introduced into the public domain until the decades following the publication of Johnson's *Dictionary*. George Campbell, in his *Philosophy of Rhetoric*, is the most thorough and thoughtful of the numerous followers of Johnson and Lowth.

Book 2 of Campbell's treatise opens with what appears to be an audacious challenge to the prescriptivists. The only "laws of the language" that can possibly obtain, he declares, are those of custom, fashion, and usage; and it is unreasonable in critics and grammarians to pretend that any other canons of grammatical excellence exist.

> What . . . shall we make of that complaint of Doctor Swift, "that our language, in many instances, offends against every part of grammar?" Or what could the doctor's notion of grammar be, when expressing himself in this manner? Some notion, possibly, he had of grammar in the abstract, an universal archetype by which the particular grammars of all different tongues ought to be regulated. If this was his meaning, I cannot say whether he is in the right or in the wrong in this accusation. I acknowledge myself to be entirely ignorant of this ideal grammar; nor can I form a conjecture where its laws are to be learnt. . . . Perhaps he meant the grammar of some other language: if so, the charge was certainly true, but not to the purpose. (140)

Anomalies and exceptions, therefore, "though departing from the rule" that governs their case, are just as legitimate as regular forms, if they are solidly rooted in custom and usage.

The object of this axiom, however, is to free the critic from rules based merely on logic and on languages such as Latin, not to undermine prescriptivism. For the nature of that "usage" which "gives laws to language" is defined in the remainder of this chapter as the usage of "those who have had a liberal education" (143), not of "the generality of people," who "speak and write very badly" (142), and not of the court, which in Britain "is commonly too fluctuating an object" (144). Modes of speech authorized by a majority of "authors of reputation," who speak not a local but a national brand of English, furnish Campbell with standards. And they must be modern authors—in a noteworthy departure from Johnsonian principles, Campbell rejects Hooker, Raleigh, and even Milton, cleaving only unto writers who flourished after 1688.

The goals of "verbal Criticism," however, are purity and perspicuity, and even the most reputable modern authors are "not uniform" in their usage; so for the next 120 pages Campbell gives rules ("canons") by which we can choose among different locutions equally sanctioned by major authors and discusses various offenses against purity and perspicuity. Clarity, simplicity, and consistency are the qualities that justify canons 1, 2, 4, 6, and 9. The opposite of these three qualities, for Campbell, is solecism (not ornateness or sublimity). Canon 1 decrees that of two possible locutions we should choose the less ambiguous (154). For example, *of consequence* means 'significant', so for a conjunction use *by consequence*. When in doubt, consult "the analogy of the language," says canon 2: though the expression, "he *used* not go; he *dare* not do it" is commonplace, it is so "exceedingly irregular" that "hardly anything less than uniform practice could authorize it" (156). Chapters 3, 4, and 6 of book 2, pages 169–214 and 216–55, are entirely devoted to solecisms of different denominations: "Barbarisms," "Improprieties," grammatical errors, obscurities, unintelligibleness, and double meaning. There cannot be any doubt as to what Campbell thinks of sloppy English.

Nor can there be question as to Campbell's disapproval of colloquialisms in good writing. "Vulgarisms," he assures us, no matter how generally accepted in common conversation, are "not reputable" (142). "Illiterate" people in common conversation make numerous "blunders" (142). Although he is unwilling to require that every acceptable word have a known etymology, he draws the line at colloquialisms and slang terms that "proclaim their vile and despicable origin" by the "disagreeable" or "frivolous" ideas associated with them, for example, *bellytimber, bamboozle, helterskelter.*

> These may all find a place in burlesque, but ought never to show themselves in any serious performance. A person of no birth, as the phrase is, may be raised to the rank of nobility, and, which is more, may become it; but nothing can add dignity to that man, or fit him for the company of gentlemen, who bears the indelible marks of the clown in his look, gait, and whole behaviour. (169)

At a number of points linguistic snobbery like this is based explicitly on the idea that spoken English is less elegant and correct than written English (143, 169, 183).

On the question of archaisms, Campbell is less ambivalent than Johnson or Lowth. It is not "prudent," he believes, to use words or phrases that cannot be found in writings published after Shakespeare (147); it is better to stick to authors published since 1688. Two of the nine canons seem to conflict in this respect. Canon 5 decrees that where no other criterion applies one should prefer the older form, such as *ye* for the nominative and *you* for the objective case (159). Canon 8, on the other hand, encourages us to dispense with old-fashioned words, especially those which occur chiefly in idiomatic expressions, for example *lief*, in "I had as *lief* go myself," and words such as *dint* and *whit* (166). The general caste of Campbell's argument is modernist, however. Canons 1 and 2 legislate against ambiguity and inconsistency, but at the same time they discredit archaisms, since about one-third of the examples of ambiguity and inconsistency Campbell gives are archaisms. The first species of "barbarism" Campbell addresses in chapter 3 is "obsolete words" such as *hight, cleped, peradventure, whenas, anon.* Such nonanalogical compounds as *selfend, selfpassion,* and *selfpractice,* wrote Campbell, "might have been regarded as flowers of rhetoric in the days of Cromwell, when a jargon of this sort was much in vogue, but are extremely unsuitable to the chaster language of the present age" (176).

Chaste as a praiseword in that last sentence is a clue to one of Campbell's distinctive achievements: he succeeds, as Johnson does not, in suggesting that prescriptivism has aesthetic elements in it. He pursues in language some of the same ideals of simplicity, harmony, and balance that we find in neoclassical architecture or in classical music. Canons 3, 4, and 6 illustrate this sensitivity in Campbell. Canon 3 advises us to prefer (between equals) the locution more "agreeable to the ear": thus, *delicacy* is to be preferred to *delicateness*, and *vindictive* to *vindicative* (158). Simplicity and brevity are the criteria for canon 4. Canon 6 rejects "harsh and unharmonious" words (162)—not, however, without a splendid footnote ridiculing Swift's antipathy to "harshness by the collision of consonants": even the most graceful languages, Campbell points out, have "many ill-sounding words," such as *splangknidzesthai* and *prosfthengxasthai* in Greek (163–64).

Let me summarize: contrary to the usual generalizations on eighteenth-century prescriptivism, English grammars before Lowth (1762) are prescriptive mostly in theory, not in practice. They pay lip service to neoclassical ideals of correctness, precision, logical consistency, and purity of language, but they give few rules or practical instructions in how to reach these ideals. It is only in the 1760s and 1770s that prescriptivism comes to fruition, and it is only the authority and perspicuity of major literary-philosophical writers (Johnson, Lowth, Kames, Campbell) that establish clear criteria for good English usage.

If good English usage is defined as formal (written) English, clear, correct, and modern, it will necessarily be the property of those who "have had a liberal education" and who have read widely among "authors of reputation" (in Campbell's words). Conversely, we may formulate a working hypothesis to the effect that most texts rich in colloquialisms, solecisms, and archaisms derive from the lower classes.

Interestingly, all conditions for this relation between syntax and social class were present as early as the 1660s, when Dryden was forming his style and standards—all but one, a detailed set of practical rules and principles for grammatical correctness. The absence of widely accepted standards of this kind explains why this hypothesis applies so inconsistently before 1760 or 1770. Dryden, Pope, and Swift, each in his own fashion, attack "vulgarity" and revise their writings in the direction of modernity, correctness, and formal precision. Defoe, whose ear for language must have been uncannily good, incorporates all the major features of lower-class English into a narrative ostensibly written by a prostitute-thief of the London streets.

But Swift himself becomes one of the principal targets of Lowth, Kames, and Campbell, berated for grammatical faults of which he was unaware; and if one goes prospecting for lower-class linguistic traits in authors between Dryden and Johnson, the results are surprising. John Bunyan, the Bedford tinker, proletarian to his fingertips, turns out to be a natural athlete of language: in Bunyan we find colorful archaisms and provincialisms, colloquial and rural expressions, but almost no solecisms at all. John Locke, who was a major philosopher, an Oxford scholar, a diplomat, physician, and scientist, writes slovenly English, especially in the *Letter concerning Education*, but also in the deservedly celebrated *Essay concerning Human Understanding* (see chapter 3). Anthony Ashley Cooper, third Earl of Shaftesbury, Locke's pupil, is well known for the ornateness of his style and should also be praised for the clarity, correctness, and modernity of his language. Both Addison and Steele are guilty of grievous grammatical faults, especially faulty reference and non-parallel construction, despite their university degrees and literary triumphs.

After 1762, however, with Johnson, Kames, and Lowth all in print, there was no reason for an educated writer to fall inadvertently into archaism, solecism, or colloquialism, if the hypothesis presented in this chapter is correct. It would be unreasonable to expect this hypothesis to be infallible or universal: natural languages in transition—which is their usual, normal state—do not operate in that fashion. But it seems to explain some of the most interesting stylistic variations in Frances Burney, Tobias Smollett, and Captain James Cook, as we shall see in chapter 3.

NOTES

1. Defoe of course has many prose styles; see Eustace Anthony James, *Daniel Defoe's Many Voices* (1972). James T. Boulton may be cited as one of many critics who feel that Defoe's colloquialism is a virtue, that too much has been made of his "clumsiness," and that at his best he is a master of "lucid, unsophisticated and unornamented, but tough and flexible prose"; see "Daniel Defoe: His Language and Rhetoric" (1965), 6–7, 10. Quotations in this paragraph are from Michael Shinagel, *Daniel Defoe and Middle-Class Gentility*, vii. Ian Watt, in *The Rise of the Novel* (1957), talks of the

vulgarity of Defoe's style. Note that the education and social status of several of Defoe's major characters are studiedly ambiguous. Moll has "a Gentlewoman's Hand" and a natural gift for genteel activities such as French and music: see G. A. Starr's edition, 13, 18 (subsequent references to *Moll Flanders* will cite this edition). Col. Jack, in the novel that bears his name, was told that his "Father was a Man of Quality" (3).

2. Richard Head, *The English Rogue*, 30–34. Editing *Moll Flanders* for the Oxford English Novels series, Starr makes effective use of B. E., *A New Dictionary of the Terms Ancient and Modern of the Canting Crew* . . . (1698), to explain "Recruit" (105) and "burnt in the hand" (86); these are slang, not cant.

3. Basic material on discourse structure was culled from Randolph Quirk, *A Grammar of Contemporary English* (1972); articles by Charles Li and Sandra Thompson, Wallace L. Chafe, and Edward L. Keenan, in Charles Li, *Subject and Topic* (1976); Joseph Grimes, *Papers on Discourse* (1978); John Joseph Gumperz, *Discourse Strategies* (1982); and Michael A. K. Halliday, *System and Function in Language* (1976). For written versus spoken discourse, see Naomi Baron, *Speech, Writing, and Sign* (1981).

4. See R. M. W. Dixon, *The Dyirbal Language of North Queensland*, 23, 70–81. On "loose, sprawling sentences that wander like a river through marshy country" in sixteenth-century prose, see James Sutherland, *On English Prose*, 7, 9–11, 44–48.

5. Thus, Early Modern English is taken to have reigned from 1500 to 1650 and to have given way to Modern English around the middle of the seventeenth century, in John Nist, *A Structural History of English* (1966), and in Albert C. Baugh, *A History of the English Language* (1957). "With Dryden and Swift the English language reached its full maturity," writes Simeon Potter in "English Language" in *The New Encyclopaedia Britannica*, 6:882–83. What seems to me far the best one-volume work on the subject, by contrast, treats the evolution of English as a continuous process: see Barbara M. H. Strang, *A History of English* (1970).

6. For the normalness of double negatives in Elizabethan English, see Baugh, *History of the English Language*, 300, 336, and Edwin Abbott, *A Shakespearian Grammar* (1872), 295. In the *Dictionary*, Johnson allows *neither* as "the second branch of a negative" but hedges over the grammaticalness of the construction. One of the examples he gives is Genesis 3:3 in the King James translation. The widespread currency of this translation (1611) operated as a powerful brake on linguistic change in certain contexts. Johnson says that he took high Elizabethan English as a standard for excellence and correctness in the *Dictionary*, which must therefore be used with caution as an arbiter for up-to-dateness. On the evolution of the auxiliaries in English, see Abbott, *Shakespearian Grammar*, 232, and Strang, *History of English*, 148–52.

7. Abbott, *Shakespearian Grammar*, 146–48. "Someone gave it me" is

still current in present-day colloquial British English. On the subjunctive and on sequence of tenses, see A. C. Partridge, *Tudor to Augustan English*, 129. On archaic subordinate conjunctions, see Wilhelm Franz, *Shakespeare-Grammatik*, 275ff., and Carey McIntosh, "The Evolution of Subordinate Conjunctions in English."

8. On *meer* and *other*, see Abbott, *Shakespearian Grammar*, 24–27. At several points in my use of the *OED* I have had to assume that archaisms play a different role in nineteenth-century literary prose from the role they play in eighteenth-century literary prose: *lo, ye deem not, many a, in good sooth she speaketh*, and similar poeticisms may be found not only in gothic fiction but also in such authors as Carlyle, used for special effects.

9. *The Works of John Dryden*, 17:21. For a valuable article discussing Dryden's "intense animus" against the language of Ben Jonson's time and his strong desire to "refine" Elizabethan syntax and vocabulary, see John Fowler, "Dryden and Literary Good-breeding," 225–46.

10. For a different perspective on the evolution of prescriptivism, see Murray Cohen, *Sensible Words* (1977), chapters 2 and 3, especially pages 60–102. Here is a list of early grammars I examined, with notes on the quantity or quality of prescriptivism they contain:

(1) 1700: A. Lane, *A Key to the Art of Letters*, 112 pages long, deals with letters and syllables (1–18), words, that is, parts of speech (18–74), and sentences (simple and compound: 74–110). Syntax for Lane is largely a matter of "the right joining of words" (76), that is, agreement. One or two prescriptive terms, such as "vulgar" and "elegant," appear on 36, 53, 60, 82, 97, 105, 108.

(2) 1707: Thomas Dyche, *A Guide to the English Tongue*, 117 pages long (plus tables of abbreviations, homonyms, and texts for copying), is principally a list of one-, two-, three-syllable words (etc.), for spelling.

(3) 1711: John Brightland and Charles Gildon, *A Grammar of the English Tongue*, follow the same scheme as Lane: letters (1–58), syllables (59–66), words (67–140), sentences (141–60). Brightland and Gildon are more interested in the philosophy of language than in correctness, refer to Locke (67) and the Port-Royal grammar (93), and add an appendix on French grammar (161–79). They prefer *who* to *which* for people, and dare to say that the King James Bible may need "many *Grammatical* Corrections" (91–92), but supply very few rules of their own.

(4) 1711: James Greenwood, *An Essay towards a Practical English Grammar*, 310 pages long, reprinted in a more popular, abridged version in 1737 as *The Royal English Grammar*, has Lane's four-part structure, except that spelling is left for the last, "letters" omitted, and etymology given its own section, 169–207. Although this seems a more substantial book than the other grammars published before 1755, it is much swollen with catechistical repetitions, quotations from authorities, digressions (e.g., on names and their etymology, 44–46, 202–7), and extracts from John Wallis

(60 pages of them). Greenwood's chapter on syntax is 6 pages long and empty of prescriptivism. He himself uses *which* for persons (214), the pleonastic *do* (48, etc.), *except* as a conjunction (47), *wrote* as the past participle of *write* (44). On page 49 he censures the archaic plurals *shoon*, 'shoes', and *eyen*, 'eyes'; on page 101 he says that double comparisons and double superlatives are not "*good* English"; and on pages 158–59 he proscribes *never so much* as a blunder, *ay* as "rude and ungentile."

(5) 1724: Hugh Jones, *An Accidence to the English Tongue*, 69 small pages. Part 1 (2–15) is on the letters, including tart remarks on dialectal pronunciation, "the various disagreeable tones of the *Common English*." Part 2 (15–19) is on syllables and roman numerals. Part 3 (20–38), on words, discusses the three [*sic*] parts of speech, and Part 4 (39–41), on sentences, discusses concord and word order quite briefly. Part 5 (41–69) is a short introduction to rhetoric.

(6) 1728: John Entick, *Speculum Latinum*, 40 pages. An attempt to teach English grammar in such a way as to prepare students to learn Latin grammar, Entick's book itself is written in old-fashioned English ("Why then call you 'em Primitives?") and has no place for rules. The last 12 pages give English analogues to Latin cases.

(7) 1734: William Loughton, *A Practical Grammar of the English Tongue*, 176 small pages. Loughton's popular book, "calculated chiefly for the Use of the FAIR SEX, and such as require only an ENGLISH Education," includes one passing remonstrance against "corrupt and wrong pronunciation" (6); also, he outlaws the "ungenteel and rude" use of *thou*, not *you*, for one person (43). He proscribes *without* as a conjunction (118) and *is it me?* (119). Elsewhere he is descriptive, not prescriptive. And his own prose has an antiquated feel to it. "*Q. Does z* ever alter its sound? *A.* No; it being always sounded *ds* or rather soft *s*, the sound of *d* being very little, if at all, perceivable" (34): a double ablative absolute.

(8) 1740: Thomas Dilworth, *A New Guide to the English Tongue*, 154 small pages. According to R. C. Alston, it was "the most popular and most frequently reprinted of the many spelling-books" of the eighteenth century. Part 3 is a short grammar (85–126); it covers capitalization, prosody, punctuation, and parts of speech, with extensive lists exemplifying each, including some odd concepts ("second future . . . as in Greek": *will educate hereafter*) but no rules in the prescriptive mode. Dilworth's own prose is archaic and rough-hewn in a country-pedagogical way: "to pronounce . . . without *Tones* or distorted *Countenances*, which *ill Habits* . . . are too frequently contracted under such bad *Methods* of Instruction, which I have endeavoured to root out: *Habits*, which, it is too true to be concealed, as it were, persecute the *Learners* . . . : For, having been accustomed to a bad *Tone* in their early Pronunciation, are scarce ever able to quit their lamentable Way of reading with *Hems* and *Hahs*" (viii).

(9) 1750: Ann Fisher, *A New Grammar*, 158 pages, thirty-five known edi-

tions before 1800. Orthography and prosody take up pages 1–64. Part 3, "Etymology," deals with parts of speech. Part 4, "Syntax," is only 11 pages long. There are some rules here, stated and implied, but relatively few: rules for agreement between subject and verb, and rules against double negatives (12) and *"Transpositions"* (127). There are "Examples of Bad English" (129–31), but they are very crude and simple-minded compared to those in Lowth: "I takes it to be;" "Them that disagree;" "the most eloquentest of all Orators" (130–31).

11. For example, on page 89 he fights language change; on page 110 he approves of "for to die." Writers and teachers, as distinguished from linguists, find it hard not to struggle against language change: even William Safire, who has no scholarly prejudices, puts his foot down on certain issues.

12. (1) *Wert* "ought not to be used in the indicative." (2) *The grammar is now printing* (which Otto Jespersen discusses as an "activo-passive" usage, *A Modern English Grammar*, 347–52) "is, in my opinion, a vitious expression, probably corrupted from a phrase more pure, but now somewhat obsolete: *The book is a printing*." (3) Subjunctive "wholly neglected" by modern writers. (4) When a verb has a past participle, distinct from preterite, use it as "more proper and elegant."

13. For "harsh," see Samuel Johnson, *Johnson on Shakespeare*, 131, 136, 137, 249; for "confused" and "perplexed" passages, 142, 255; for archaisms explained (not censured), 324, 150, 151; for colloquialisms, 251, 458. The word *vulgar* in Johnson may carry only its etymological meaning, 'pertaining to the common people', not its pejorative meaning, as on page 458. Johnson was conscious that Shakespeare's grammar was looser and less regular than eighteenth-century grammar; "concerning Shakespeare's particles [= prepositions, conjunctions] there is no certainty" (477, and see also 314).

CHAPTER TWO

Courtly-Genteel Prose

T HE PURPOSE of this chapter is to identify a way of writing
that I call *courtly-genteel prose*, to describe its distinctive character and functions, and to trace its lineage. It will become clear,
and even incontrovertible, given the origins of texts quoted and
their purpose and use, that courtly-genteel prose has close associa-
tions with upper-class society of the seventeenth and eighteenth
centuries.

Courtly-genteel prose borrows terms from the specialized vocabulary of the courtier and uses them to be polite with, to create
verbal elegance independent of the court or of any specific noble or
royal person. Its forms and formulas go back to the fifteenth century or earlier; remnants of them survive in the twentieth. It is the
language of dependency, courtship, petition, dedication, honor,
unsalaried service, friendship, and prayer.

A defining characteristic of courtly-genteel prose is its reliance
on a small number of abstract, almost technical terms derived from
the social environment of the court. A courtier, simply by being a
courtier, is *obliged* to *serve* his noble lord, part of whose responsibili-
ties in turn are to extend *favor* to those of his henchmen who *deserve* it and to confer *honor* in return for suitable quantities of *merit*.
In this relationship, superior and inferior alike have an *interest* in
maintaining a balance between *duties* owed and *obligations* incurred.
We recognize courtly-genteel prose by its reliance on the words italicized here, plus a few related ones. They are the names of vari-
ables in terms of which status is conferred and manipulated; they
are verbal counters for the politics of dependency. Since the *will* or
pleasure of a noble lord dominates the court, much of the action in
courtly-genteel prose is subordinated to these two abstractions or to
other more splendid attributes of the sovereign in question, to his
or her *goodness*, to "his *grace*" or "her *majesty*." *Will* and *pleasure*
make themselves known as motivations of a noble lord in the predi-

cate of courtly-genteel sentences; other abstractions may serve as subject or benefited object: "His *grace* is willing to permit . . ."; "Please accept grateful acknowledgments of the *favor* and benefits your *goodness* has conferred on me."

Courtly-genteel prose may be found in abundance between roughly 1550 and 1800 in any of six general contexts where its use became obligatory or customary: (I) in the language of diplomacy and petition; (II) in love and courtship; (III) in letters of high friendship; (IV) in courtesy books and books of model letters; (V) in dueling handbooks and in the flowery prose of chivalric romance; (VI) in homily and prayer. Since literary and linguistic histories of English have not recognized the pervasiveness of courtly-genteel language, and since its importance in literature and as a medium for class consciousness depends on a recognition of its central position in at least these contexts, this chapter will include more quotations than it might otherwise. Sections I–VI below document each of these contexts in turn.

Obviously, these categories overlap. Letters of petition, in section I, and letters of courtship, in section II, may both be found also in the books of model letters of section IV. The correspondence between noble or noble-minded friends in section III may closely resemble letters of courtship between high-minded lovers in section II. Courtesy books, in section V, advised people not only on polite behavior but also on polite language, and sometimes gave directions for writing such petitions and letters as might properly appear in sections I, II, and III. Many of the best-known and longest-lived passages in the Book of Common Prayer (section VI) take the same form as petitions to much lesser lords in section I. The heroes and heroines of romances in section V are almost by definition lovers (as in section II), courtiers (as in section I), and friends (as in section III).

On the other hand, it is probably the diversity of texts cited in this chapter that explains why courtly-genteel language has not been identified as a distinct style hitherto. Examples of courtly-genteel locutions as employed by a practicing courtier or diplomat are plentiful in the letters of Sir Philip Sidney (1554–86) or Sir William Temple (1628–99) or the Earl of Chesterfield (1694–1773) and in most dedications of literary works published between 1550 and 1800—but literary and linguistic historians seldom have occasion to lay these texts side by side with passages from the Book of

Common Prayer or with quotations from the multivolume heroic
and courtly romances that were fashionable in mid-seventeenth-
century France and England. The original contexts for courtly-
genteel prose were not literary. The diplomat was a professional, or
(more accurately) a dedicated gentleman-amateur, who expressed
himself in courtly-genteel language because it was the language of
his function (section I). Most books of model letters (section IV) are
distinctly subliterary, like model business letters in writing text-
books today. Quoted in this chapter, however, are literary passages
from minor fiction of 1609, 1613, 1623, 1705, 1720, and 1723 as
well as from *Pamela* (1740) and *Joseph Andrews* (1742), and from
plays dated 1651 and 1677 as well as from *Macbeth* (1603). The central predicament of Richardson's novel *Clarissa*, as well as the style
of many of Clarissa's letters, is courtly and genteel. The diversity of
texts cited in this chapter counts as an argument in support of my
thesis that courtly-genteel prose may be associated with upper-class
aspirations in general, not merely in specific literary genres.

Courtly-genteel prose is a reminder of a precommercial system
of dependencies that required one human being to place him- or
herself so completely at the disposal of another as to be considered
(verbally, at any rate) to belong to him. Thus, William Paston, the
lawyer who between roughly 1420 and 1440 accumulated land and
money on which later Pastons based their respectable position as
gentry in fifteenth-century Norfolk, petitions the Vicar of Cluny:

> Whereupon I pray you with all my heart, and as I may do
> you *service*, that it *like* to your *grace* to grant of your *charity*.
> . . . And that it *like* you overmore ['moreover'] to accept
> and admit the said resignation by your authority and
> *power*, with the *favour* of your good *lordship* in comfort and
> consolation. . . . And I am *your* man, and ever will be. (1:1;
> my italics, as throughout ch. 2)

"I am *your* man"; for purposes of this petition, in other words, 'I
depend on you as vassal depends on feudal lord'. There is no evidence that William Paston had ever committed himself personally
or legally to the Vicar of Cluny as retainer or servant much less
taken the oath that bound vassal to feudal lord; nevertheless, in this
letter Paston appeals for the Vicar's *favor* and signs himself "*your*
man."

Since the original function of courtly-genteel prose seems to have been not so much to express sentiments as to forward transactions—the granting of a favor or honor—its use extended down the socioeconomic scale to whoever could write a petition, and up the scale to the royal family itself. In or about 1506, long after his royal authority had been established more thoroughly and solidly than had that of any fifteenth-century king, Henry VII wrote to his mother, Margaret, Countess of Richmond, in the verbal equivalent of a sweeping bow of obeisance:

> Madam, my most entirely wellbeloved Lady and mother, I recommend me unto you in the most *humble* and lowly wise that I can, beseeching you of your daily and continual blessing. . . . And my Dame, not only in this but in all other things that I may know should be to your *honor* and *pleasure* and weal of your soul I shall be as glad to *please* you as your heart can desire it, and I know well that I am as much *bounden* so to do as any creature living. (*Original Letters*, 1:43–44)

According to Marc Bloch (231–33), the vassal-to-lord relationship spread through feudal society into groups for which extreme obedience and fealty were not inherently necessary: children became vassals to their parents in the eyes of the law, lovers were vassals to their ladies, men to God (hence the custom of praying with folded hands, after a rite of homage where the lord takes the hands of his vassal in his).

Over the centuries, courtly phrases of submission and devotion lost the strict, even legal significance they may have carried in a feudal age, and dwindled into formula. We still in the fourth quarter of the twentieth century end letters routinely with the scraps or petrified remains of courtly-genteel locutions. "*Yours* truly" and "Sincerely *yours*" preserve the grammatical signs of a relation between noble lord and "his" humble servant that is hundreds of years out of date. The word *please*, as in "Please pass the salt," is also a fossil of ritual allusions in courtly-genteel prose to the *pleasure* of one's lord or master: "May it please your Lordship" or "Be pleased to pass the salt."

Not that the more or less feudal relationships from which courtly-genteel prose seems to have derived were total anachron-

72

isms in the seventeenth and eighteenth centuries. Johnson and Boswell traveled to the Hebrides in 1773 to see a country where "the feudal institutions [had recently] operated upon life with their full force," and everyone paid "rent and reverence" to the laird (Johnson, *Journey*, 65, 86). A significant amount of land in eighteenth-century England belonged to people not by *freehold*, which was what we would consider legal ownership, but by *copyhold*, a tenancy for a specified number of years or for life, associated with rents and services. Landed aristocracy dominated British politics and upper-class social life even after the American, French, and Industrial revolutions had made their mark. A full set of social values, alternative to the traditional ones which placed court and noble lords at the top of a broad pyramid based on landless labor, scarcely existed before 1800, except among such radical Protestants as the Quakers. Feudalism itself may have faded out in the thirteenth century or later, but social relationships modeled after the feudal system of obligations and duties, honor and service, lingered on. In particular, as this essay will demonstrate, it survived in the language of courtly-genteel prose.

I. THE LANGUAGE OF DIPLOMACY AND PETITION

According to one authority, the fundamental principles of feudalism include "mutual *obligations* of loyalty, protection, and *service*." "The faithful performance of all the *duties* he had assumed in homage constituted the vassal's right and title to his fief." The tenure by which a thing of value was held was "one of *honourable service*, not intended to be economic, but . . . [rather], seeking the lord's *interests*," or giving the lord advice in feudal courts. As feudalism originated in a general need for "protection against the sudden attacks of invaders or revolted peasants," against excessive or illegal demands by the government itself, so "feudalism disappeared . . . when a professional class arose to form the judiciary, when the increased circulation of money made regular taxation possible and enabled the government to buy military and other services" (Adams, 206).

Real vassals pledging fealty to real feudal lords are therefore rare in the seventeenth and eighteenth centuries, except in fiction.

DUNCAN: Would thou hadst less *deserved*,
                That the proportion both of thanks and payment

> Might have been mine! Only I have left to say,
> More is thy *due* than more than all can pay.

MACBETH: The *service* and the loyalty I owe,
    In doing it, pays itself. Your Highness' part
    Is to receive our *duties*, and our *duties*
    Are to your throne and state, children and *servants*,
    Which do but what they should by doing everything
    Safe toward your love and *honor*.

(Macbeth, I, iv, 18)

The couplet ending Duncan's speech identifies it as something official and ceremonious. Coleridge saw in Macbeth's courtly reply "nothing but the commonplaces of loyalty," the product of "exceeding effort"—which is plausible in the light of Macbeth's aside, twenty lines later, confessing to "black and deep desires." It is as if Shakespeare chose courtly-genteel language as a proper medium to express the most public, honorable devotion, so that the contrast between Macbeth's words and his thoughts could be as complete as possible.

By 1600, courtly-genteel prose had become, among other things, an identifying trait for the species or type of human being called *courtier*. Thomas Dekker, in *The Gull's Horn-Book* (1609), admonishes the aspiring confidence man,

> If you be a courtier, discourse of the obtaining of suits, of your mistress's *favours*, etc.; make enquiry if any gentleman at board have any suit, to get which he would use the good means of a great man's *interest* with the King. (94)

A hundred and twenty years later the same locutions furnish material for the same kind of jest in Henry Fielding's burlesque play *The Author's Farce* (1730):

> SPARKISH: What dost think of the play?
>
> MARPLAY: It may be a very good one for aught I know; but I know the author has no *interest*.
>
> SPARKISH: Give me *interest*, and rat the play.
>
> MARPLAY: Rather rat the play which has no *interest*. *Interest* sways as much in the theatre as a court, and you know it is not always the companion of *merit* in either. (26)

In passages like these, the vassal/lord relation has degenerated into petty jockeying for place.

By my best estimate, about 90 percent of all dedications to works published between 1550 and 1750 use courtly-genteel language, probably because the major pecuniary benefits of authorship before Pope and Richardson were owing to patronage and the patron's favors, not to commissions or sales. Dedicators therefore felt *obliged* to proclaim how little they *deserve* or *merit* the *honor* of the *favors* of their dedicatees, etc., etc.

> Sir, I am both by alliance your poor Kinsman, by sundry great courtesies your *debtor*, & by your exceeding travails taken in my behalf, I am become *yours bounden* and assured. So that it shall be my part with full endeavor so to employ my time, as I may either countervaile or *deserve* some part of your bountiful dealings. (2:3)

This is George Gascoigne throwing his *Glasse of Governement* at the feet of Sir Owen Hopton in 1575. Similar statements, high-flown but rather empty, issue from the pen of John Ford in 1633 in the dedication of *'Tis Pity She's a Whore*:

> Your noble allowance of these first fruits of my leisure in the action emboldens my confidence of your as noble construction in this presentment; especially since my *service* must ever *owe* particular *duty* to your *favours* by a particular engagement. (87)

Sentiments like these were echoed in the prefatory matter to a thousand publications as long as there was anything substantial to be got out of a patron. They are couched in courtly-genteel language even when addressed to a nonaristocrat, being essentially petitions for favor.

It is important to recognize, however, that courtly-genteel prose is not restricted to occasions when material favors and appreciable honors are at stake. Viscount Beaumont had written in 1454 to John, Lord Lovel, his son-in-law, petitioning for a stewardship for one of his dependents. In this transaction Lord Lovel is the patron, Beaumont the suitor on bended knee, but Lovel's reply seeks to reverse this relationship:

Howbeit, my Lord, your *desire* shall be had in all that is in
me; and at the instance of your *Lordship*, I, by the advice of
my counsel, shall give it him in writing, under such form
as shall *please* you, wherein I would be glad to do that that
might *please* your good *Lordship*, praying you right heartily
ye would be mine especial good lord and father in all such
as ye can think should grow to my *worship* or profit in any
wise, as my singular trust is most in you. And I alway [*sic*]
ready to do you *service* with God's *grace*. (*Paston Letters*,
1:136)

Having conferred the favor that Beaumont requested, Lovel does
his best to escape from the position of noble lord, at least verbally;
he reverts as quickly as he can to vassalage, at least on the textual
level. I deduce that courtly-genteel phrases were employed as often
to establish attitudes as to make transactions: just those attitudes
that are common to all the major contexts that will be documented
in this chapter, ceremonious humility, perfectly attentive to the *interests*, the *will* and *pleasure* of the addressee. Hence the prominent
role of courtly-genteel locutions in texts aspiring to courtesy and
politeness.

Diplomats used these locutions in their official correspondence
in order to maintain both a respectful attitude and a posture of petition: by definition, in this period, a diplomat is a courtier seeking
to pry advantages and favors out of the noble lords who govern for-
eign states. In the absence of telephone, telegram, and television, a
written correspondence between a diplomat and his inferiors and
superiors was the primary medium for negotiation from a distance.
Thus, the Earl of Chesterfield writes in 1729, petitioning for a
change of post:

When I had the *honor* of seeing his *Majesty*, I had not time
to beg permission to pay my *duty* in England, where not
only my own inclinations call me . . . but where also my
own private affairs render my presence necessary. I must
therefore beg of your Lordship to use your *interest* with his
Majesty that he will be *pleased* to give me leave. (2:136)

Chesterfield has a specific purpose here. Elsewhere, diplomats use
courtly-genteel prose to further the cause of correspondence for its

own sake, as is clear from some of Sir William Temple's letters to the Duke of Ormond (1:218–19).

The novelists appropriated courtly-genteel phrases to give their characters a varnish of politeness. Thus a quite ordinary lad in a perfectly undistinguished novella of 1613 is elevated in dignity as follows:

> He put his fortunes on towards the Morotopian Court, where it *pleased* the pages of the nobility to do him much *favor*, and the ladies to *grace* him with the *honor* of knight-ship. (Anton, *Moromachia*, 57)

Similar language appears routinely in lesser romances of the time, slatternly narratives, many of them, trying to capitalize on the perennial popularity of stories of fine heroes and romantic love. In *Luck at Last; or, The Happy Unfortunate* (1723), Sylvia tries on the courtier's verbal mannerisms as a shopkeeper's girl may try on milady's silk taffeta:

> I am sure I am *obliged* to my good lady here, and to all her good family, and should be glad to *serve* them. . . . Sylvia humbly thanked Angelica for the *honor* she did her and promised to do her utmost to *merit* her *favor*. (Black-amore, 40, 45)

Among numerous accomplishments that Richardson's Pamela picks up during her years as a domestic servant is courtly speech, which she turns to good effect as a way of expressing her total dependency on her newly affianced lord and master:

> In the first place, sir, if you will give me leave, I will myself look into such parts of the family economy, as may not be beneath the rank to which I shall have the *honour* of being exalted, if any such there can be. . . . And when you shall return home from your diversions on the green, or from the chase, or where you shall *please* to go, I shall have the pleasure of receiving you with *duty*, and a cheerful delight. . . . Both the means and the *will*, I now see, are given to you, to lay me under an everlasting *obligation*. How happy shall I be, if, though I cannot be worthy of all

this *goodness* and condescension, I can prove myself not
entirely unworthy of it. . . . If ever I give you cause . . . to
be disgusted with me, may I be an outcast from your
house and *favour*. (276, 277, 279)

Perhaps one reason some modern readers look askance at Pamela
is the super-genteel way in which she abases herself before her
husband.

The fact that these quotations end in the eighteenth century
should not be construed to mean that courtly-genteel prose was
never employed in the nineteenth century. But this brand of verbal
gentility began to sound old-fashioned as the Industrial Revolution
hit its stride. Courts and courtiers waned in importance after 1800,
and literary patronage faded in significance. Not much effort, however, I believe, would be needed to produce examples of courtly-
genteel locutions in nineteenth-century dedications, petitions, and
letters couched in the spirit of an earlier age. Political patronage, if
we may judge by a letter of Edmund Burke written in 1782, fell
quite naturally into the phraseology of earlier forms of patronage
sponsored by the court:

Dear Sir, May I beg the *favour* of your vote and *interest* for
Mr Webb Member of Parliament for Gloucester to be a di-
rector of the East India Company. He is a friend of mine
whom I wish very much to *serve*. I am with very great truth
and regard, Dear Sir, Your most obedient and humble *Servant*. (5:31)

II. LOVE AND COURTSHIP

Until twenty or thirty years ago, a man trying to persuade a
woman to marry him was referred to as a *suitor*, and his collective
behavior was called *courtship*. Until about two hundred years ago,
this same man was often known as his lady's *servant*, and much of
the terminology of courtly dependencies was redeployed within the
language of love. Ironically, this form of courtship is a chapter in
the history of the subjection of women. Having been flattered with
absolute power to grant *favor* or withhold it (a power severely limited by convention and circumstance), a woman was chained to her
pedestal and restricted to passive, unanimated behavior. The man
ostensibly bound to her *service* was in practice free at any time to

get up off his knees and act. The extravagant dependency he imputed to himself in his courtly-genteel rantings was a social fiction.

Relations between the sexes is one of two areas of experience where the vocabulary of the courtier has been degraded, over the centuries, by what etymologists call concretization. At least three key courtly terms have dwindled into sexual euphemisms. It is possible to talk about a woman's *honor* and refer to nothing more spiritual than the virginal membrane. *Favors* may mean sexual intercourse and nothing more. A stallion is said to *service* a mare. By a flanking movement in the realm of manners, four courtly terms have been trivialized, losing their high chivalric gloss, into physical objects or etiquette-words; a lady's *favor* was a glove or a scarf, a belonging she could bestow on her lover as emblem of her love; *courtesy* evolved into the act of bending the knees and bowing the head (also, since about 1575, spelled *curtsey*); and to pay one's respects to someone, usually bowing at the same time, was to pay one's *duty* or make an *honor* to him or her.

The other area is of course finance. An *obligation* was "the action of binding oneself by oath, promise, or contract . . . an agreement whereby one person is bound to another," as early as 1297; pecuniary "obligations" according to the *OED* date from 1382. The commercial and the courtly senses of *owe* are intertwined from Anglo-Saxon times on (see *OED*, s.v. "owe," B, II, 2); and to *pay* someone is to give him or her what is due to him or her in money *or* service, from the thirteenth century on. We still talk of money, goods, and *service* as properly coordinated terms. Debts of *honor* are still acknowledged in their sphere as taking priority over the kind of debt one owes to a bank or a hardware store, and the most dishonorable cheat in the nation may still be capable of *honoring* a debt.

Any number of texts will illustrate the use of courtly-genteel prose in amorous discourse between the sexes. An entire love affair is condensed into four sentences by the irrepressible Thomas Nashe, whose hero seems to employ courtly-genteel terminology mostly because he is in such a hurry to be off on his travels again that he wishes to avoid discussion of real affection:

> Seeing her, I admired her; all the whole receptacle of my sight was inhabited with her rare worth. Long *suit* and uncessant protestations got me the *grace* to be entertained.

> Did never unloving *servant* so prentice-like obey his never
> *pleased* mistress as I did her. . . . I most *humbly* besought
> her of *favor* that she would give me so much *gracious* leave
> to absent myself from her *service* as to travel a year or two
> into Italy. (*The Unfortunate Traveler*, 233, 234)

We know this is a love affair because it uses the technical terminology proper to courtly love in the debased form that lasted so
long in popular literature—certainly not by any signs of affection,
respect, or personal engagement.

It seems to be the case, in general, that lower-class popular fiction steers clear of courtly-genteel language, but middle-class
popular literature cultivates it extensively as a way of elevating the
status of lovers and refining their sentiments. Thus, Thomas
Deloney (1563–1600), by trade a silk-weaver, whose narratives are
tuned to an artisan-shopkeeper mentality, hardly wets his little toe
in the reservoirs of courtly-genteel prose. It is noteworthy that he
uses it at all, as in such formulaic replies as, "Sir (quoth she) I confess your love *deserves* a Lady's *favour*, your affection a faithful
friend" (128). I found similar traces or residues of the courtly vocabulary in *Amadis of Gaul* (1592, 3r, 3v), the popular and durable
tale of secular chivalry and violent adventure, but no traces or residues in samples of the equally popular *Seven Champions of Christendom* (1596), though its two heroes are also knights in armor. An
eighteenth-century lower-class tale, *The Jamaican Lady* (1720),
chronicles an aborted shipboard affair as follows:

> He only hopped half a dozen times round the cabin, made
> an awkward *honor*, and so completed his minuet . . . But
> whether she was as willing to receive as he to offer his *ser-
> vice* I know not, or whether she imagined loss of *honor* con-
> sisted only in the discovery. (90, 108)

W. H. McBurney classifies this novel as pseudo-picaresque (xx); it
demonstrates how far from the court courtly terminology spread,
being a ragamuffin narrative both in style and substance.

Genuine love in Fielding's low-class heroes (e.g. Joseph Andrews) expresses itself without benefit of courtly-genteel phrases.
When Betty the house-maid develops a sudden crush on Joseph,
during his recuperation, she "swore he was the handsomest Crea-

ture she had ever seen." The blue-blooded Lady Booby, on the other hand, dresses her erotic impulses in thoroughly courtly style:

'Joseph, have you so much more sense and so much more virtue than you handsome young fellows generally have, who make no scruple of sacrificing our dear reputation to your pride, without considering the great *obligation* we lay on you by our condescension and confidence? . . . Suppose you should have any wicked intentions upon my *honour*, how should I defend myself?' . . . 'Indeed, madam,' says Joseph, 'I will never do anything to *disoblige* your ladyship.' . . . 'And yet, Joseph,' returned she, 'ladies have admitted their footmen to such familiarities; and footmen, I confess to you, much less *deserving* them . . . Would you be contented with a kiss? Would not your inclinations be all on fire rather by such a *favour*? . . . Intolerable confidence. Have you the assurance to pretend, that when a lady demeans herself to throw aside the rules of decency, in order to *honour* you with the highest *favour* in her power, your virtue should resist her inclination?' (22, 23, 32)

In *Tom Jones* (1749), social class helps to determine which lover draws on this repertory of courtly locutions and which does not (see ch. 3).

Quotations in the preceding paragraphs illustrate the conventional language of courtship and very little else. But many authors writing about love seem to take the same vocabulary seriously. A man truly in love is in fact exceedingly dependent on the will and pleasure of his beloved and wishes to serve her. Her favor is priceless, her honor something he reveres. We can see the dingy outlines of a serious accommodation between the language of love and the language of the courtier, couched in courtly-genteel terms, in one of Delarivière Manley's lower-middle-class bodice-rippers, published in 1705:

As Hippolito is a brave man, he will scorn to be *obliged* long to a woman, who having first forfeited her *honour* to her royal master, will cancel the *obligations* of *honour* he otherwise *owed* to her, and be glad of the pretense to bestow his *favours* on another woman, in whose beauty and fidelity he can place his heart as well as his *interest* . . . [His passion] is proof against all other batteries of *duty* or *interest*. (*Queen Zarah*, 1:10, 14)

The syntax is confused; slightly amended, it tells us that Hippolito is genuinely enough a "brave man" to jilt a woman who has "forfeited her honour" to someone else, even the king, and to seek out another woman in whose "fidelity" his "heart" can trust. His love for her will be proof not only against "interest" but against "duty" itself as well.[1]

III. LETTERS OF HIGH FRIENDSHIP

Just as the correspondence of diplomats was more important before telegram and telephone arrived than it is now, so the correspondence of friends, in those ages when travel was arduous, played a far larger part in personal or social relationships as a whole than it does at present. Furthermore, modern readers will require an effort of the imagination to appreciate the value of friendship itself in those early years. That Cicero's *De Amicitia* was one of the most popular books of the Renaissance, widely used as a school text, and frequently translated, must have had something to do with the fact that friendship was considered a virtue, not a mere social relationship; or rather, friendship was conceived as the love of virtue in another person and therefore as a powerful, even inspiring aid to virtue in oneself.

Hence evolved a context within which the extreme humility and exalted devotion of courtly-genteel prose was perfectly at home. In the correspondence of true friends, each professes himself or herself overwhelmed by the *obligations* that some abstraction (the *goodness, generosity, courtesy*, etc.) of the other has placed on him or her; neither will admit to *deserving* such *favors*; whatever *services* they perform fall short of each other's *merit*.

In letters of elegant friendship from 1500 to 1800, something very like the following sentiments, as expressed by Thomas More in 1517, turn up again and again:

That in your letter you thank me so carefully for my *services* on behalf of your friends is a mark of your great *courtesy*. What I did was quite trifling: it is only your *goodness* that exaggerates it. But you scarcely do justice to our friendship, for you seem to think that what I may do puts you under an *obligation*, whereas you should rather claim as your own and *service* due you. (19)

One's correspondent's gratitude is interpreted as a sign of his or her virtue as a friend, and one's own gratitude as something less than what was due. A letter in a book of model letters of 1658 by Milton's nephew, Edward Phillips, starts out, "I must complain of the excess of your civilities and curtesies," and protests that the friend should not thank him "for curtesies received from me, as if I were not *obliged* to do them" (130, 129). Alexander Pope, at nineteen, launches a correspondence with Sir William Wycherley in the same terms:

The compliments you make me, in regard of any inconsiderable *service* I could do you, are very unkind, and do but tell me in other words, that my friend has so mean an opinion of me, as to think I expect acknowledgment for trifles; which upon my faith I shall equally take amiss, whether made to my self, or to any others. For God's sake (my dear friend Wycherley) think better of me, and believe I desire no sort of *favour* so much, as that of *serving* you, more considerably than I have yet been able to do. (1:33)

Wycherley was a noble lord, older and well established in the literary world, so that Pope's letter of high friendship may also be read as a letter to a potential patron.

High friendship is the medium in question here, not chumminess, not the intimacy of pals or buddies. Women were not excluded from such friendships, and the letters of such extraordinarily intelligent and lively women as Elizabeth Carter and Hester Thrale express the ardent modesties and enthusiastic humilities of high friendship ("romantic" in the same sense as the heroic romances of the précieuses) in courtly-genteel terms. Perhaps the most influential model of an epistolary style that combined dignity, upper-class perspectives, and courtly-genteel preoccupation with patronage and friendship, however, is the celebrated 1746 translation of Pliny's letters by William Melmoth:

I am extremely anxious for the success of the petition which Euritius has presented to the Senate; and I feel for my friend what I never felt for myself. My credit and character, are indeed, in some measure at stake. I obtained for him of Caesar the *honour* of wearing that Laticlave, and also the office of quaestor; as it is by my *interest* too that he is *indulged* with the privilege of petitioning for the Tribunate. . . . But if I were not for these reasons *obliged* to *interest* myself in the success of Euritius, yet his probity, good sense, and learning would incline me to assist him with my utmost power; as, indeed, he and his whole family are *deserving* of the highest commendation. His father, Euritius Clarus, is a man of strict *honour*. (1:82–83)

The Loeb Classics editor, praising Melmoth's ease and felicity of style, made this translation the basis of his. The passage quoted here has special interest not only because of its characteristically eighteenth-century elegance but also because most of its courtly-genteel vocabulary is Melmouth's invention, with no equivalent in the Latin.[2]

IV. Courtesy Books; Model Letters

I have argued so far that precommercial dependencies between vassal and lord are a prime source of the courtly-genteel terminology of *service, favor, honor, interest* and *obligation*; that courtly-genteel prose was standard equipment for petitioner and diplomat between roughly 1450 and 1800; and that love and high friendship, which were noncommercial dependencies of a different order, adopted courtly-genteel language to their own purposes. We are now in position to look at two species of books that increased the circulation of courtly-genteel prose, bridging the gap between court and marketplace, popularizers through which middle-class readers and writers might have gained familiarity with the language of courtly patronage and service.

Courtesy books

The term *courtesy books* refers to a genre as characteristic and popular between the Renaissance and the Industrial Revolution as

84

how-to-do-it books are now. The *New Cambridge Bibliography of English Literature* lists 162 separate titles of courtesy books for the years 1660–1800 (see also Mason, 1935). Didacticism was not something shied away from in this period, which inherited the medieval fondness for "sententious" writings, and a great many didactic writings in the sixteenth through eighteenth centuries have close affiliations with courtesy books. The books of model letters discussed below are a variety of courtesy book, and so are works of fiction pretending to exemplify "virtue not angelical, nor above probability" (as Johnson puts it in *Rambler* 4), sermons on domestic matters, and some periodical essays (e.g. *Tatlers* 107 and 116; *Spectators* 16 and 57; *Ramblers* 72 and 98). Swift and Fielding wrote essays on "polite conversation." The most popular book (except the Bible) of our period, *The Whole Duty of Man*, seeks out single-mindedly to tell common folk how to behave in their daily lives so as to fulfill their domestic and social duty as Christians.

The Book of the Courtier, Baldassare Castiglione's classic work translated by Thomas Hoby in 1561, dwells more on the spirit than the letter of courtesy, so that courtly-genteel terminology is thinly scattered in its pages: the courtier is advised in one place to "accompany all his motion with a certain good judgment and *grace*, if he will *deserve* that general *favor* which is so much set by." Later on we are told that "to purchase *favour* at great men's hands, there is no better way than to *deserve* it" (41, 109). Another Continental courtesy book of considerable influence, *The Civile Conversation of M. Steeven Guazzo*, translated by George Pettie in 1581, initiates us into the world where clever, well-turned compliments are essential to polite speech:

> it is not amiss to follow the example of that discreet gentleman, who, after long strife between him and certain of his friends, who should first enter into the house, saith, You may now know well how much I am at your command, seeing I am ready to obey you in things which turn to my *dishonour*: which said, he entered in without straining courtesy any longer. (1:166)

Act 3 scene 5 of James Shirley's *Love Tricks* (1625) has its own subtitle: "The Complement-School," and parodies courtly-genteel compliments:

"God save you, sir; felicities be accumulated upon you, sir;
I thank you, generous sir; you *oblige* me to be your *servant*,
sir, in all my —p—o—s—possibility, sir: I *honour* your re-
membrance, sir, and shall be proud to do you my obser-
vance, sir." (51)

As late as 1752, Rousseau refused a pension for fear of the embarrassment he anticipated from replying to the king with one of his
"usual inanities" instead of a polite compliment like the one just
quoted (*Confessions*, 354).

Few courtesy books, however, are quite as explicit about mas-
tering a repertoire of courtly language as that by "the Scottish
Chesterfield," Adam Petrie, who in 1720 recommends frankly that
"when you meet with elegant and ornate sentences, write them
down, and labour to have them imprinted in your mind." Petrie
supplies examples of courtly-genteel discourse:

When you speak of what your superior did for you, or you
heard from him, you must say, *You did me the honour, You
was pleased to put your self to the trouble to tell me so. . . . May I
presume to desire the favour of your doing so and so.*

Such instructions may have been more needed in Scotland than in
London; at any rate, Petrie elsewhere feels it necessary to rebuke a
pedestrian for "wagging his Breech" and for staring at "one easing
Nature" (59, 65, 66, 7, 9).

Model letters

Collections of model letters suitable for all occasions were published in substantial numbers from the sixteenth century on.
William Fulwood's book, *The Enimie of Idleness* (1568), for example,
is a hefty volume, 290 pages long, with detailed instructions about
forms of salutation and subscription appropriate to superiors,
equals, and inferiors, as well as model letters in verse and prose,
samples from the epistles of famous men, mirthful letters, angry
letters, love letters. Here and in early seventeenth-century model
letter books such as *Cupids Schoole* (1632), we find courtly-genteel
mannerisms mainly in letters of petition.

By the middle of the seventeenth century, however, any letter
with serious pretentions to politeness was likely to include courtly-

genteel language. In *The Academy of Complements* of 1640 appears the following well-mannered if semantically empty little note:

> Sir, This my *duty* shall confirm the rest, which I desire to yield you by my *service*. With this request, that you hold me still in your remembrance, as him that shall never affect other *merit* than that of obeying you, whereby to be by you esteemed, Sir, The most obedient of all, Your *servants*. (180)

According to the *New Cambridge Bibliography of English Literature*, this book reached a twelfth edition in 1663. Vincent Voiture's letters were translated into English as early as 1657 by John Davies; and by the time John Dryden translated some of them for a successful collection of *Familiar and Courtly Letters* in 1700, they had become a model not only for polite language ("you do me too much *honour* to think of me at all") but also for a species of courtly badinage cultivated by Pope and Swift.

This mine of courtly-genteel language was not exhausted for at least a hundred years. The model letters best known to students of the novel appear of course in Samuel Richardson's *Clarissa* (1748), "a series of letters . . . between two young ladies of virtue and honour, bearing an inviolable friendship for each other" (author's preface, 1759). Richardson wrote his own book of model letters, too, almost as calisthenics for his first novel, and it abounds with courtly-genteel phraseology:

> Honoured Sir, Permit me to approach you with the thankful acknowledgements of a grateful heart, on the *favour* and benefit your *goodness* has conferred upon me. It shall be the business of my whole life, to the utmost of my power, to *deserve* it; and my whole family, which you have made happy by your bounty, will every day join with me in prayers to God, to bless you with the continuance of your valuable health, a long life, and all worldly *honour*; for so it will become us to do, for the *unmerited favours* conferred upon, *honoured* sir, Your most *dutiful Servant*. (140–41)

Katherine Hornbeak found letters from Richardson's collection reprinted as late as 1916! And, of course, model letters are still being published in such best-selling contemporary courtesy books as Emily Post's and Amy Vanderbilt's volumes on etiquette.

V. Chivalric Romance

It is not an accident that some of the terminology of courtly-genteel prose plays a role in a book about dueling published in 1602. Dueling has always been a matter of *honor*. Thus,

> The ancient emperours . . . had in use to bestow upon captains and soldiers certain gifts to encourage them to *serve* well . . . If he were a horseman, he received an ornament or *favour* to be set on his crest. . . . These donations or *favours* did not only encourage men to valour, but also made them much *honoured* at home. . . . [Book II, chapter 7:] The office and *duty* of every knight. . . . [Book III, chapter 14:] Of *honour* gained or lost by being disarmed. . . . [An Italian testimony translated into English:] Philip by the *grace* of God King of France . . . to every other person that take delight or pleasure in arms . . . to the end *honour* may be given to every one according to his *merit*. (Segar, 27, 60, 100, 185–86)

In the world of chivalry, all courtiers are knights, and all knights are courtiers, and dueling is one of their major functions. Duels were not in our period just bloody quarrels but a duty of the upper-class male, whose rank in society, which was as much part of his identity as his name or his ancestry, expressed itself equally in semi-feudal attitudes toward property, including land and women, in use of the sword, and in courtly-genteel language.

Whether this was always true in historical fact or not, it was certainly true of the high chivalric romances that dominated English and French prose fiction and heroic drama for at least a hundred years after Sir Philip Sidney's *Arcadia* (1590). Seventeenth-century chivalric romance synthesized courtly values that are elsewhere divided among the duelist or soldier, the lover, and the courtier or gentleman: heroes of these interminable narratives are equally adept in love and war.

Exalted heroism and trebly idealized love, however, call for prose styles raised correspondingly high above the everyday norm;

and so courtly-genteel mannerisms are relatively unobtrusive when incorporated into the spangled prose of chivalric romance. We are so dazzled by conceit, hyperbole, alliteration, and the rest of the poetic apparatus of these narratives, that courtly-genteel phraseology does not stand out.

> After that by your means I was exalted to *serve* in yonder blessed lodge, for a while I had, in the furnace of my agonies, this refreshing; that (because of the *service* I had done in killing of the bear) it *pleased* the princess (in whom indeed stateliness shines through courtesy) to let fall some *gracious* look upon me. Sometimes to see my exercises, sometimes to hear my songs. For my part, my heart would not suffer me to omit any occasion, whereby I might make the incomparable Pamela see how much extraordinary devotion I bare to her *service*: and withall, strave to appear more worthy in her sight; that small *desert*, joined to so great affection, might prevail something in the wisest lady. But too well (alas) I found that a shepherd's *service* was but considered of as from a shepherd, and the acceptation limited to no further proportion than of a good *servant*. (153)

Sidney's *Arcadia*, from which this passage is taken, was a minor masterpiece in the genre of heroic romance, a genre that influenced drama as deeply as it did fiction.

The fact that most modern readers find most of these plays and novels unreadable may be owing in part to occasional over-dependency on courtly-genteel language, as in these tangled lines from Thomas Killigrew's ten-act *Cicilia and Clorinda* (1651):

> The *honour* I have had to know your Highness makes me not doubt the receiving this satisfaction, that I may at least preserve my *honour*, though the rash Cicilia has falsely prophaned hers. [Amadeo decides to accept the challenge,] . . . to show how much I loved the Princess, and how little thou [Lucius] *deservest* to be preferred before me. Sure no man of *honour* could ever have thought he should have occasion to draw his sword in the defense of the Princess Cicilia's *honour* against one that knew her. . . .

Otho, too, ungrateful Otho, all my *services* thrown by, has *interested* himself in my ruin, and has chid, and threatened his sister to her *dishonour*. (257, 267, 268)

The word *honor* occurs in almost every major speech in this sprawling tragicomedy. I confess to a lurking fondness for the colossally noble sentiments of John Phillips's translation of *Pharamond*, by Gautier de la Calprenède (1677), whose heroes are so extravagantly courteous, and whose courtesy is so superlatively heroic, that one begins almost against one's will to believe in them. In the opening scene of this gargantuan tale, a band of Romans under Constance meet Pharamond and friends; naturally they joust, without parley; naturally Pharamond wins; and then they talk, and talk, and talk:

—Great Sir, (said [Pharamond]), do not at all regard those as enemies of your nation, who cannot be so of virtue; and though we have fought against the Romans in defence of our liberty, yet do not believe that you shall find among them more respect and more *service* than you shall among persons who have for a long time been *honourers* of your far-famed glories.

—If the Romans (replied Constance) are so unfortunate, as to have many enemies like you, I shall fear their empire will be much endangered; but when I should be less *obliged* to that noble entertainment you give me, I see in you things so great, and so little common, that no *interest* of nations whatsoever can be capable to render me your enemy: but if you can pardon the curiosity of a person who in the estate he at present is hath no reason to demand, *please* you to let me know to whom I am *obliged*, for so noble and generous proceeding.

—My name is Pharamond (answered the Prince) and I am—

—'Tis enough (said Constance, interrupting him) by the name of Pharamond, you tell me all things, yet possibly nothing more than I knew before: for to be what you appear to our eyes, 'tis necessary that you must be Pharamond, whose renown the world publishes amongst its greatest wonders.

—That renown (Pharamond modestly replied) has been

too partially *favourable* in the recital of our actions; but I shall be sufficiently *obliged* to it, if it has given me any place in your esteem, and that I can hope that you and your companion will not refuse to take here some few days of repose, and suffer those wounds to be dressed, which by the blood upon your armour I guess you to have received. (6)

From one point of view all these passages celebrate the values of an earlier age. Segar's book on dueling is largely a compilation of cases and anecdotes from a hundred years before, or more. Killigrew's play and de la Calprenède's novel are both fantasies about a long ago and far away that never happened.

Dueling, however, is still not extinct, and the language of codes of honor lasted longer than the codes themselves. Literary historians continue to underestimate the power that chivalric romance exerted on attitudes, values, and codes of behavior—including verbal behavior—during the seventeenth and eighteenth centuries. Clara Reeve's two-volume dialogue on *The Progress of Romance* (1785) treats the Scudérys and de la Calprenède with respect, remarking, however, that they "produced a particular kind of affectation in speaking and writing" (66). Reeve is probably referring to seventeenth-century précieuses, but no student of the novel can afford to ignore the influence of romanciers whom most of us will never read on the imagination of novelists whom all of us read, Richardson, Fielding, and Smollett (S. Baker, 1964, 1961).

VI. Prayer

Some petitions from the fifteenth century sound like prayers: the Earl of Marche and his brother wrote to their father, Richard, Duke of York, in 1460,

Right high and right mighty Prince, our full redouted and right noble lord and father, as lowly with all our hearts as we your true and natural sons can or may, we recommend us unto your noble *grace*, humbly beseeching your noble and worthy *fatherhood* daily to give us your hearty blessing: through which we trust much the rather to increase and grow to virtue. . . . We thank our blessed Lord not only

of your *honourable* conduct and good speed in all your
matters and business, and of your *gracious* prevail against
the intent and malice of your evilwillers, also of the knowledge that it *pleased* your nobility to let us now late have of
the same. (*Original Letters*, 1:9)

Richard is their "lord" whom they "humbly beseech" for a blessing,
and to whose *grace, fatherhood, honor*, and *pleasure* they pay tribute.
 On the other hand, many prayers are petitions, addressed to a
lord whose honor and glory are theological, not political, facts.
Bishop Joseph Hall dedicated a sermon preached in April of 1609
in such a way as to combine the language of dedication, prayer, and
petition:

> To the only *honour* and glory of God, my dear and blessed
> Saviour, which hath done and suffered all these things for
> my soul, his weak and unworthy *servant* humbly desires to
> consecrate himself and his poor labours: beseeching him
> to accept, and bless them to the public good, and to the
> praise of his own glorious name. (5:22)

People familiar with Christian traditions are so accustomed to hearing of the *honor* and glory of God, his *service*, his *grace* won by the
merits of Jesus, that they do not make the connection between religi-
osity and courtesy signaled by this language. That it is not a universal connection may easily be demonstrated by a look at Hindu
prayers or American Indian prayers, or by reference to a religious
formula that is free from western courtly ties, "There is no God but
Allah and Muhammed is his prophet," which is at least as important in Moslem worship as any single phrase in the Christian liturgies. Similarly, an address to one of God's attributes, his goodness,
mercy, or loving kindness, seems to us almost inevitable in prayer,
and everywhere in the collects of the Book of Common Prayer such
abstractions are set up as motives or agents, just as other abstractions are in courtly-genteel prose.
 The Book of Common Prayer, first published in 1549, was revised in 1596, 1662, and other years, and its collects as currently
used in Anglican and Episcopal churches remain in most instances
word-for-word the same as in Thomas Cranmer's version of 1549.
Revisions at least through 1920, for example, have left courtly expressions in the following prayers untouched:

O Lord and heavenly Father, we thy humble *servants* . . .
earnestly desire thy fatherly *goodness*, mercifully to accept
this our sacrifice of praise and thanksgiving; most humbly
beseeching thee to grant, that by the *merits* and death of
thy Son Jesus Christ, and through faith in his blood, we,
and all thy whole Church, may obtain remission of our
sins, and all other benefits of his passion. . . . And although we are unworthy through our manifold sins to offer unto thee any sacrifice; yet we beseech thee to accept
this our bounden *duty* and *service*, not weighing our *merits*,
but pardoning our offences . . . O God, . . . whose *service*
is perfect freedom, defend us thy humble *servants* . . . Al-
mighty God, who has given us *grace* at this time with one
accord to make our common supplications unto thee, . . .
fulfill now, O Lord, the desires and petitions of thy *servants* . . . O Lord, we beseech thee *favourably* to hear the
prayers of thy people . . . Give us *grace* to use such absti-
nence, that . . . we may ever obey thy Godly motions . . .
to thy *honour* and glory. . . . everlasting God, which . . . art
wont to give more than either we desire or *deserve*.

Additional examples of courtly-genteel language in Christian liturgy may be found among the prayers published specially for use
in the reign of Elizabeth I.[3]

VII. The Ancestry of Courtly-Genteel Prose

A proper history of courtly-genteel language would have to
come to terms with sources and analogues in Latin and French.
Then it would have to unravel threads of affiliation in Middle English among the three chief medieval forms of obligation and service—feudal, amorous, and religious—since all three call on a
vocabulary that has much in common with the polite phrases of
seventeenth- and eighteenth-century courtly style. It would illustrate successive stages of the changes that took place in this cluster
of special terms and idioms between Chaucer and Shakespeare. It
would have to try to show that what appear to be artificial conventions of salutation, appeal, and valediction in formal and familiar
epistles are related to real-life dependencies of these three kinds.
What I offer here is not a proper history but a set of sketches for
backgrounds before about 1560.

The terminology of courtly-genteel prose has its equivalents in Latin. *Favor* and *gratia* correspond to "favor" in English, *gratia, obsequium*, and *servitium* to "service." To have an obligation to someone can be *homini gratiam debere*, and to honor someone may be expressed as *honorem habere alicui*. The *Thesaurus Linguae Latinae* says that *obsequium* is used for honoring and saluting (most commonly in epistles): *honorando vel salutando* (*maxime in epistulis*). Du Cange's *Glossarium ad Scriptores Mediae et Infimae Latinitatis* records for *servitium* a family of meanings similar to what the *OED* records for "service": church services, service at table, feudal obligations, service of institutions, people, and ideals. Letters in classical Latin observe the distinction between "love earned by service" (*officioso amore*) and "spontaneous" love (*amor fortuitus*). Jean Leclerq has shown that a tradition of epistolary conventions runs unbroken from classical times to the Renaissance. The Latin Middle Ages worked out elaborate formulae for beginning and ending letters to superiors: *princeps sue fidelitatis servicium tam debitum quam devotum* is one of dozens in which the ideas of honor, duty, obligation, and service play a part. Medievalists seem to agree that highly ornamental salutations and farewells in very early English letters are patterned after the formulae prescribed in books of *dictamen*, but many of the same words crop up also in a book such as *De amore* (The Art of Courtly Love) by Andreas Capellanus, which tells how a lover makes plans to "find *favor* with" his beloved (*Incipit enim cogitare, qualiter eius gratiam valeat invenire*), and instructs a middle-class man to offer himself and "his services" to "her grace" (*me et mea vobis offerre servitia vobisque supplicare attente, ut ea dignetur suscipere gratia vestra*) (30). It seems safe to say that a thorough investigation of the language of patronage, dependency, and friendship in Latin would uncover styles and conventions comparable to courtly-genteel prose in English, in slightly different configurations.[4]

Courteous and courtly prose in sixteenth- and seventeenth-century France shows some striking family resemblances to courtly-genteel English. In a letter to the Cardinal de la Valette, July 1621, Guez de Balzac writes:

> Je voudrois bien vous pouvoir remercier assez dignement de cette *faveur*, mais outre que vos bien-faicts sont trop grands, et que vous *obligez* de si bonne *grace*, qu'elle en augmente encore la valeur, je serois presomptueux si je

94

croyois que les paroles que je vous pourrois dire fussent du prix des actions que vous faictes. . . . Puis que je trouve mon *interest* dans mon *devoir*, il faut de necessité que je vous ayme, si je ne me hay moymesme. . . . Toutesfois ce n'est pas ceste derniere consideration qui m'attache le plus á vostre *service* . . . Je regarde donc vos bonnes *graces* toutes nues; et l'estime que vous faictes de moy, m'est une *obligation* d'autant plus chere que les autres, qu'elle considere mon *merite*, et non pas ma pauvreté. (1:92−93)

There is nothing raw or unformed about this, and if it is representative, the language of compliment and honor must have reached full maturity in France by the 1620s, in time to influence English directly through Charles I's French wife and during Charles II's exile. In note 5, selections from letters by Michel de Montaigne (1570), from letters in Honoré d'Urfé's *Astrée* (1607), and from the argument and text of Pierre Corneille's *Clitandre* (1632) illustrate a few of the varieties of courtly-genteel prose in French. Since a sizable proportion of seventeenth-century English courtesy books and romances were translations from French, it is possible that polite French should be counted as one of the most influential ancestors of the language of courtesy in eighteenth-century England.[5]

What do we learn from a sampling of English before 1560 that helps us understand how courtly-genteel prose evolved? Literary works may deal with courts and kings and knightly lords and ladies of honor without making extensive use of courtly-genteel prose. In Thomas Malory's *Morte d'Arthur* (1485), the courtly-genteel vocabulary is drastically reduced. *Duty* is wholly absent, *honor* and *favor* appear hardly at all, a knight's *interest* and *obligations* are never discussed, and Arthur's *pleasure* or *will* seems not to count for enough to deserve mention. One reason for this certainly is the unwillingness of Malory's knights and ladies to talk about themselves at any length. Gareth asks a boon of Arthur without referring at any point to honor or service, merit or favor:

'Now, sir, this is my petition at this feast, that ye will give me meat and drink sufficiently for this twelve-month, and at that day I will ask mine other two gifts.'
'My fair son,' said king Arthur, 'ask better, I counsel thee, for this is but a simple asking; for mine heart giveth me to thee greatly, that thou art come of men of *worship*, and

greatly my conceit faileth me but thou shalt prove a man
of right great *worship*.'
'Sir,' he said, 'thereof be as be may, for I have asked that I
will ask at this time.' (213)

In another passage Tristram recalls the bond that ties the Table
Round to their king:

'My fair fellows, wit you well that I will turn unto king
Arthur's party, for I saw never so few men do so well. And
it will be *shame* unto us that bene knights of the Round
Table to see our lord king Arthur and that noble knight,
sir Lancelot, to be *dishonored*.'
'Sir, it will be well done,' said sir Gareth and sir Drynadan.
(565)

Few words and to the point. In a fifty-page section of book 6, the
following relatively relaxed courtly locutions appear:

And some . . . knights increased in arms and *worship*.
(180)

So this sir Lancelot increased so marvellously in *worship*
and *honour*. (180)

Wherefore queen Guinevere had him in great *favour*
above all other knights. (180)

Gramercy, fair damsel, of your good *will*. (183)

By the faith of my body, your father shall have my *service*.
(185)

Would ye promise me of your *courtesy* . . . for to cause him
to be made knight? (186)

Therefore, while that I live, I shall do her *service* and all
her kindred. (187)

If that ye have need any time of my *service*, I pray you let
me have knowledge. (189)

Now damsel, will ye have any more *service* of me? (194)

There shall ye yield you unto queen Guinevere and put
you all three in her *grace* and mercy. (197)

'That were *shame* unto thee.' . . . 'Thou gettest none other
grace.' (206)

96

This shall I do for to please you: ye shall have homage and *feawté* and of an hundred knights. (231)

Malory's considerable powers as a literary stylist have not much to do with the conventions of courtly-genteel prose that I have been discussing in this chapter.

The vocabulary of courtly-genteel prose changes at different times and in different authors. The 1927 concordance of Chaucer records only 18 occurrences of *favor* but more than 250 of *grace*. One of the abstractions around which Arthur's court heavily wheels in Malory, *worship*, has almost completely disappeared from the courtly lexicon of the eighteenth century, except as a specialized honorific of address. In *worship*, notions of honor and fame are combined with notions of honorableness, integrity, and skill in fighting: "the more he is of *worship* the more shall be my *worship* to have ado with him" (228). By continuous jousting some knights "increased in arms and *worship* that passed all other of their fellows in prowess and noble deeds" (180). Cador of Cornwall welcomes an insolent message, "for now shall we have war and *worship*" (137); that seems a little bloodthirsty, but Malory never pretends that his knights lead an easy life.

Honorific abstractions cannot by themselves generate a courtly prose style. This is borne out in the Paston letters of the sixteenth century, which deploy a number of such novelties to make themselves more polite but do not thereby succeed in making themselves more elegant:

Beseeching your good *mastership* that. (1:65)

Thanking you evermore of your great gentleness and good *masterhood*. (1:85)

I recommend me unto your good *motherhood*. (1:133)

Thanking right heartily your good *brotherhood* for your good and gentle letters. (1:11)

The style of the letters from which these ingenuities are quoted is plain and homely. In many of the Paston letters and in the *Morte d'Arthur*, the formulae of courtly service and honor subsist quite unpretentiously in a world of blunt physical urgencies, where there is no need for tactfulness or a subtle counterpoint of relationships.

In other words, apart from those diplomatic documents, letters, petitions, and dedications for which courtly-genteel language is

standard operating terminology, the polite and high-born locutions
that have been the subject of this chapter are not introduced into
the prose of middle-class and upper-middle-class writers, or into
literature, until the later sixteenth century. At that time the combined force of the Book of Common Prayer (1549), the first English
courtesy and model letter books (1568), and chivalric romances
from Italy and France made the entire paraphernalia of courtly-
genteel prose available to anyone who could read. After about
1650, the enormous prestige of French literary culture and politeness and the continued rise of an increasingly literate middle
class domesticated courtly-genteel language into such a familiar
phenomenon that its frequent usage in letters, in plays, and as a
mark of social class in such novels as *Tom Jones* and *Clarissa* has
never been noticed.

VIII. SUMMARY

What I have chosen to call courtly-genteel prose, to distinguish
it from other varieties of courtly language on the one hand and
from genteel discourse on the other, may be identified by its reliance on about a dozen key terms in the lexicon of the courtier: his
obligation to provide appropriate *service* to his lord, in return for
such *honor* and *favor* as he may *deserve*. These and a few other
terms, for example, *interest, merit,* and *duty,* are subordinated or
governed both metaphorically and grammatically by the abstract
virtues of the noble lord in question, his *grace,* his *goodness,* his *majesty.* They have close analogies, perhaps ancestors, in the traditional
polite formulas of Latin letters from late classical times to the Renaissance, and in French courtly prose of the sixteenth century.

The origin of courtly-genteel prose, however, is probably not
literary but social or (in the broadest sense) political, since a version
of feudal dependency is one element in common among all its six
or eight major contexts; the writer or speaker projects an attitude
of extreme subservience, humble service, faithful devotion. We find
numerous examples of courtly-genteel language in petitions and
dedications, and in the correspondence of courtier-diplomats such
as Sidney and Chesterfield. We also find it in fiction and drama
where an author wishes to imitate the courtier's manner of speech
to express attitudes of polite respectfulness.

Friendship and love are contexts within which extravagant
submissiveness makes personal or emotional sense. In courtship,

the lover becomes his lady's humble *servant* and seeks to *deserve* her *favor*. In high courtly friendship—a tradition that has died out in the twentieth century—each of two friends vows with great earnestness that he or she does not *merit* the *honor* of the other's *favors*. In seventeenth- and eighteenth-century fiction, the lower-class lovers do not use courtly-genteel language, but gentry and nobles do, especially those heroes and heroines who aspire to higher social rank.

Courtly-genteel prose figures largely in the books of model letters that were so popular in the sixteenth, seventeenth, and eighteenth centuries, less largely in courtesy books themselves. Again, this species of courtly language is associated with middle-class aspirations to gentility in authors such as Samuel Richardson. Heroic romance, a literary fad of some importance in the seventeenth century (though known to most readers primarily as Don Quixote's bane), incorporated courtly-genteel locutions into its fantastic narratives of an exquisitely well-bred chivalry. This was of course the age of the Three Musketeers, and all gentlemen were potential duelists, whose code of honor makes use of courtly-genteel terminology. Finally, in the Book of Common Prayer, where subservience and devotion to a more than feudal lord are perfectly appropriate, we find courtly-genteel language woven unobtrusively but unmistakably into the liturgy.

How reliable is courtly-genteel prose as an index of social class? Moderately so, I think, when used with understanding of the texts in question, their goals, origin, and sociocultural context. Of course, a cat may look at a king: any clown with wit to mimic courtly-genteel vocabulary and syntax could give the appearance at least of gentility if not of nobility. Conversely, members of the landed aristocracy did not necessarily use courtly-genteel formulas except as the message required that medium or except as the medium required that style. In uncorrected, unliterary documents such as the *Verney Letters*, which have been transcribed directly from autograph eighteenth-century manuscripts, gentry and servants write equally uncouth English, before 1725. Thus we find in a letter by Cary Lady Gardiner:

> I need not tell you . . . whot return shee has had for her
> dull and unpleasing Life shee led ther. I am sure you wod
> A bin glad if your Master had don something for all mine
> at his death, but I loved him as my Life, as well as ever sis-

ter could love A brother, & all mine was bred up to love
him as a Father. (1:17–18)

The absence of courtly-genteel mannerisms, in other words, does
not tell us anything about social class. The presence of courtly-
genteel mannerisms indicates at least a degree of concern for politeness and decorum, and in some contexts a set of assumptions
about honor, service, duty, and merit that makes no sense apart
from certain feudal relationships chiefly preserved by courts and
landed aristocracy.

NOTES

1. For distinctions between the original traditions of courtierlike behavior and courtly love, see Alexander J. Denomy, "Courtly Love and
Courtliness" (1953). For further examples of courtly-genteel jargon in the
language of "love," see George Pettie, *A Petite Pallace* (1576), 16, 17, 18,
22, 26; *Morindos* (1609), 6, 18, 20; Eliza Heywood, *Philidore and Placentia* (1727), 161, 166, 168; and Dorothy Osborne, *The Letters of Dorothy
Osborne*, 3, 8.

2. For the kind of idealized friendship in question here, see Melmouth's
translation of Cicero, *Laelius* (de Amicitia); for more samples of courtly-
genteel prose in letters of high friendship, see Sir Philip Sidney, *Complete
Works*, 3:128; Elizabeth Carter, *Memoirs*, 1:181; Elizabeth Carter, *Letters*,
1:16–18. There was certainly some tension in the eighteenth century between the desiderata of familiar and of courtly epistolary style; for the
easy, natural simplicity that many familiar letters aimed at, see Rosemary
Cowler, "Shadow and Substance," 38–39, and Cecil Price, "'The Art of
Pleasing,'" 92–93.

3. See *Liturgies*, ed. W. K. Clay (1847). For analogies between service of
God and service of a feudal lord, see Marc Bloch, *Feudal Society*, 1:231–33;
D. S. Brewer, "Courtesy and the *Gawain*-Poet"; David L. Jeffrey, "The
Friar's Rent." See also Stella Brook, *The Language of the Book of Common
Prayer*.

4. For general remarks on classical Latin letters, see Marcus Cornelius
Fronto, *Correspondence*, 1:84–89. For two traditions of medieval letters, one
passionate, the other functional, see Frank C. Gardiner, *The Pilgrimage of
Desire* (1971). For Latin formulas of salutation and valediction, see Ludwig
Rockinger, *Briefsteller und formelbücher*, 1:209–346, especially 263. See also
Katherine Gee Hornbeak, *The Complete Letter-Writer in English*, 2.

5. "Et en toute façon, ce me sera tousjours *honneur* de pouvoir faire
chose qui revienne à vous ou aux vostres, pour l'*obligation* que j'ay de vous
faire *service*"; "je vous presenterois autant volontiers quelque chose du

mien, en recognoissance des *obligations* que je vous doy, & de l'ancienne *faveur* & amitié que vous avez portée à ceux de nostre maison. Mais Monsieur, à faute de meilleure monnoye, je vous offre en payement une tresasseuree *volonté* de vous faire humble *service*" (*Montaigne*, 1362, 1367).

"Vous ne voulez croire que je vous ayme, & desirez que je croye que vous m'aymez: se je ne vous ayme point, que vous profitera la creance qui j'auray de vostre affection? A faire peut estre, que ceste opinion m'y *oblige*? A peine, Celadon, le pourra ceste foible consideration si vos *merites*, & les *services* que j'ay receus de vous ne l'ont peu encores." "Amour le vouloit, . . . son *devoir* le luy commandoit. . . . Puis que ceste *faveur* est la premiere que j'ay obtenue . . ." "Si mon affection ne vous a peu rendre mon *service* agreable, ny mon *service* mon affection . . ." (d'Urfé, 496–500).

In Pierre Corneille's *Clitandre* (dedication dated 1632), the Argument makes mention of Rosidor's "*faveur* auprès du roi," and notes that a rival's "offres de *services* sont aussi mal recues que par le passé." In act 1, a lover addresses his own eyes: "si jamais vos fonctions propices / A mon coeur amoureux firent de bons *services*, / Apprenez aujourd'hui quel est votre *devoir*." Rosidor "occupe mes pensées, / Et par le souvenir de ses *faveurs* passées," hopes to find "moyens de *plaire* à cette belle" (170, 171, 178, 179).

CHAPTER THREE

Applications

THE KEY words of courtly-genteel style, *service, favor, honor, merit, duty, interest*, and a few others, in a context of high devotion or respect, may serve reliably to indicate that a given passage of English has upper-class aspirations, affiliations, or sources. Isolated instances of any one of these key words, of course, have no necessary upper-class connections at all, as when a sea captain tells us that "By the favour of a hard gale of wind, we got clear" (1726: *OED*). All these words have acquired noncourtly meanings and contexts unrelated to social class. But in the eighteenth century even casual use of one or two of these key words, where patronage or friendship or courtship is involved, fosters a courtly tone, as even a casual quotation from Shakespeare in an otherwise pedestrian text may foster a literary tone. Thus Boswell's use of courtly-genteel words when gossiping about Johnson's pension evokes aristocratic relationships (quite different from those associated with twentieth-century pensions and pension plans): "the pension was not a *favour* but a reward *due* his *merit*"; "Johnson took it as a *favour*" and said, "'I am pénétré with his *Majesty's goodness*'" (Boswell, 55).

By contrast, solecisms, archaisms, and colloquialisms are not perfectly reliable indicators of low-class language, for a number of reasons.

(1) Great as was the authority of major prescriptivists, they were anything but unanimous on particular questions of grammar and usage. S. A. Leonard's long appendix charting disagreements among such scholars as Buchanan, Robert Baker, Campbell, Johnson, Lowth, Murray, and Noah Webster is misleading in that it pits early authorities (including Shakespeare and Defoe) against late (Webster), ignorant schoolmasters against scholars, and mainstream traditionalists against such eccentrics as Baker and Horne Tooke; but the fact remains that numerous questions of correct

usage were never definitely settled in the eighteenth century or in the nineteenth or twentieth either. (Natural languages are changeable and ambiguous enough so that no amount of authority or logic will ever decide all questions of correctness, no matter how isolated the linguistic environment may be.) For example, Lowth advocated the possessive with gerunds (*its being observed*), but Webster disapproved, as did G. Harris (see Leonard, 265).

(2) The English language was changing during those fifty or hundred years when prescriptive canons were formulated and propagated, with unpredictable results. Some words and some usages that had seemed modern and correct in 1755 seemed outmoded in 1795. Since language is "the most massively resistant, the most nearly self-determining, of human conventions" (Sledd and Kolb, 33), many of these changes would have taken place regardless of what prescriptivists wrote. Some rules were for all practical purposes washed up on shore by the tide of linguistic evolution and left abandoned by living speakers, for example Johnson's distinction between verbs active and verbs neuter, the latter of which take *be*, not *have*, in the perfect tense (James *was arrived* in town; *Dictionary*, b 1 v).

(3) Conversely, archaisms, or what we now by hindsight recognize as archaisms, lingered on in many kinds of discourse long after we might suppose that they had been banished. Language change occurs not only irresistibly but also irregularly, inconsistently, and at different rates in different contexts; it is a mistake to think that Early Modern English, which flourished in Shakespeare's lifetime, was abruptly displaced in 1660 by Present-day English. Thus, as late as 1795 Lindley Murray (in perhaps the most widely-read English grammar of all) sanctions the Elizabethan negative ("I touched him not"), imperative ("Awake ye"), proto-progressive ("To go afishing"), *and which* clauses, *had/had* conditionals, and *exceeding* for *exceedingly* as intensifier (*English Grammar*, 86, 89, 138, iv, 131, 103).

(4) Some of the most refined writers were never taught all the rules that prescriptive grammarians laid down, or chose to ignore them. Jane Austen is not uniform in applying singular adjectives to plural nouns ("these sort of things"), or in using the comparative between two alternatives ("to determine whether pleasure or pain bore the greatest share") (*Pride and Prejudice*, 139, 337).

(5) Solecisms and colloquialisms were generally considered more acceptable in informal discourse than formal, and writers

whose public productions are scrupulously correct may stoop to less elegant diction in private journals or familiar letters. Thus Joseph Spence, professor of poetry at Oxford, writes to his mother from Europe in 1731 and 1737:

> we always fall a laughing. (38)
>
> we had an extreme hard winter here. (38)
>
> not near so agreeable as. (36)
>
> otters . . . were excelent good. (40)
>
> a box . . . in which the storks build a great nest and sit very comfortably in it. (167)
>
> some of the brass-work is mighty neat. (172)
>
> we . . . had like to have met the Dutchess. (180)

Thus Johnson's friend Hester Thrale, in her *Family Book* (see Hyde, 1977), writes:

> a very good Book; . . . but it is monstrous dull Fun. (49)
>
> take me these two little Girls away. (153)
>
> went to the Baker for his Roll and watched the drawing it out of the Oven. (151)
>
> it burns special well. (150)
>
> we were all to go shew him the Tower forsooth. (150)

Archaisms and colloquialisms in Spence's letters and Thrale's journal are not a sign of low social status but of informality.

(6) Solecisms may occur when a writer attempts to express difficult ideas, regardless of his or her social class. Concepts that are refractory or hard to express may find themselves Englished in incorrect grammar. There are passages in Locke's *Essay concerning Human Understanding* that defy parsing. Everything "contained" in the "abstract idea" which we designate by the "name" of a "sort," says Locke, is its "essence."

> This, though it be all the essence of natural substances that we know, or by which we distinguish them into sorts, yet I call it by a peculiar name, the nominal essence, to distinguish it from the real constitution of substances, upon

which depends this nominal essence, and all the properties of that sort; which, therefore, as has been said, may be
called the real essence. (2:57; bk. 4, ch. 6, par. 2)

Either the verb should be plural, *depend*, or the grammatical and
logical relation of *properties* to the rest of the sentence is obscure.
Neither of the two *which*'s that follow is as unmistakably connected
to its antecedent as censorious grammarians would desire them to
be. "As has been said" sounds as though the author were a little dis-
organized in his thoughts. Locke is struggling here with difficult
ideas and with language to express them clearly.

(7) Conversely, the absence of solecisms does not infallibly
mark upper-class language but may rather be the result of un-
taught dexterity. John Bunyan, the tinker, stumbles into solecism
less often than John Locke, the philosopher. In a four-thousand-
word sample of *Grace Abounding* (1666), only five passages occur
where perfect clarity would require amendment. One of them is a
relative pronoun slightly removed from its antecedent, and this is
in fact a conjunctive locution sanctioned by the very best writers of
the seventeenth century. Two more depend on rules for sequence
of tenses that were still being established in that century. The other
two depend on the location of correlative conjunctions. On the
playing fields of language, Bunyan is perfectly at ease, a natural
athlete, despite his rural origins and lack of formal education.

All caveats considered, however, it is still possible to generalize,
cautiously, about lower-class language in the fifty or more years
after Lowth. The remainder of this chapter samples passages from
literary and nonliterary works that seem to confirm the hypotheses
presented above.

I. HAWKESWORTH'S REVISIONS (1773) OF CAPTAIN COOK (1770)

James Cook (1728–79), the son of a Yorkshire day laborer, received only as much education as the village school of Great Ayton
could offer, except in mathematics; he owed his rapid rise through
the ranks of merchant and naval services to leadership qualities
and to his genius as a navigator (Cook, cvi–cvii). His journal of the
voyage of the *Endeavour* (1768–71) to Tahiti and New Zealand was
not written for publication but composed as "the usual document
that a commander in the naval services was directed to prepare for

the official inspection of his superiors" (Cook, cxciii). It was edited and rewritten for *An Account of the Voyages . . . for Making Discoveries in the Southern Hemisphere* (1773) by John Hawkesworth, Johnson's well-educated friend and imitator. Although Hawkesworth has been accused of inaccuracy, of unnecessary editorializing, of salaciousness, impiety, and indolence, he never meets lower-class language in Cook but he removes it: that is, wherever solecisms, archaisms, or colloquialisms occur in Cook's journal, they have been either corrected or excised in Hawkesworth's *Account*. There is nothing illiterate or scabrous about Cook's journals; "the spelling . . . and construction are generally those of a man formally uneducated though of vigorous mind" (Cook, ccii). But the contrast between plain homespun in Cook and silk-and-brocade in Hawkesworth is very clear.[1]

Thus, of the perilous route through Torres Strait Cook wrote,

> one need hardly wish for a better was the Access to it from the Eastward less dangerous, but this difficulty will remain untill some better way is found out than the one we came, which no doubt may be done was it ever to become an object to be look'd for. (391)

Hawkesworth rewrote this as,

> better would not need to be desired, if the access to it, from the eastward, were less dangerous: that a less dangerous access may be discovered, I think there is little reason to doubt, and to find it little more seems to be necessary, than to determine . . . (3:619)

Gone is the old-fashioned conditional, in its place an *if* clause with the correct form of the verb, the subjunctive. Gone is the unspecific and possibly inaccurate abstraction "difficulty," and the common verb *found* gives way to the slightly more genteel *discovered*. Gone is "the [way] we came"—*to come a way* is a bourgeois idiom at best and could be accused of redundancy (cf. Campbell's scorn for "He sings a good song," 167). Gone is the ambiguous *which* referring to an entire event, not to a single substantive; gone is the awkward repetition of "be done . . . become . . . be look'd for."

What is printed here as a solecism might have been perfectly acceptable in Elizabethan English; both archaisms and solecisms appear more frequently in colloquial than in written English. With this proviso, I list Cook's lower-class locutions under these three headings, beside Hawkesworth's politer version of the same passages.

Solecisms

1. Pronoun reference

Cook	Hawkesworth
he however never landed upon it probably he was discouraged from it by the natives killing 3 or 4 of his people. (274)	but being attacked by the natives soon after he came to an anchor . . . he never went on shore. (3:435)

2. Relative pronoun separate from antecedent

Another custom they have that is disagreable to Europeans which is eating lice a pretty good stock of which they generally carry about them. (124)	as they live in a hot country, and have no such thing as a comb, they are not able to keep their heads free from lice, which the children and common people sometimes pick out and eat: a hateful custom, wholly different from their manners in every other particular. (2:191)

Note that Hawkesworth, on his own initiative, differentiates between "the children" or "common people" and upper-class Tahitians so far as lice-eating goes.

3. "No nominative" (Lowth's term)

these they tye round their necks the thrum'd side out and are generaly large enough to cover the body. (272)	one of them is tied over the shoulders with a string, and reaches as low as the knees. (3:454)

4. PARALLEL CONSTRUCTION AND AGREEMENT

which gave me no small sat-
isfaction not only because
the dangers and fatigues of
the Voyage was drawing
near to an end, but by being
able to prove . . . (390)

not only because the dan-
gers and fatigues of the voyage were drawing to an end,
but because it would no
longer be a doubt whether
. . . (3:619)

We were told of her coming
and that she would bring
with her some of the Stolen
things. (102)

we received a visit from
Oberea, which surprised
us not a little, as she
brought with her none of
the things that had been
stolen. (2:151)

5. AGREEMENT

neither us nor Tupia could
understand one word they
said. (305)

neither we nor Tupia
understood a single word.
(3:493)

when we landed now there
were no body to be seen.
(305)

which we now found totally
deserted. (3:495)

The situation of few parts
of the world are better determined than these Islands
are. (274)

which is now determined
with uncommon exactness.
(3:435)

6. IRREGULAR VERBS

they throw'd two darts at us.
(305)

he threw a lance at us,
and his comrade another.
(3:493)

the body of Vandiemens
land ought to have bore due
south. (299)

the body of Van Dieman's
land ought to have borne
due south. (3:483)

7. MISCELLANEOUS EXPRESSIONS, OFTEN OMITTED BY HAWKESWORTH

But neither this, nor the runing 14 Leagues to the South,
nor the seeing no land . . . could satisfy Mr. Gore but what

he saw in the morning was or might be land. (254; omitted
by Hawkesworth, 3:415)

Lowth would have required the gerund to take the possessive case,
both for its agent and its object. The sequence of tenses is wrong
here; 'what he *had seen* in the morning' is more accurate.

we found the soil every where except in the Marshes to be
light white sand and produceth a quantity of good grass.
(307)

For perfect correctness, this needs either an infinitive after the *and*
or a subject for *produceth*, itself the old-fashioned form of third person singular present.

Archaisms

1. PLEONASTIC *do*

The excuse she made was that her gallant, a Man that used to be along with her, did steal them and she had beat him and turn'd him away. (102)	She said indeed, that her favourite Obadee, whom she had beaten and dis- missed, had taken them away. (2:151)

Johnson called this extraneous auxiliary "a vitious mode of speech"
(*Dictionary*, b 2 v). *Did* in that sentence not only derives from Early
Modern English usage but also covers up for the more correct sequence of tenses, which Hawkesworth supplies in its place. Also
archaic are the use of *used to* for 'was accustomed to', the undifferentiated past participle of *beat*, and *that* used as relative pronoun
for people.

2. RELATIVE PRONOUNS

and Tupia and his servants both of which fell a sacrifice to this unwholsom climate. (441–42)	Tupia, and Tayeto his boy. All but Tupia fell a sacri- fice to the unwholesome . . . (3:723)

seeing no land but that we had left. (254)	seeing no land . . . but that which we had left. (3:416)

3. *Which* AS CONJUNCTION

it is discovered before you are abreast of it which you cannot do in coming from the northward. (311)	discovered before the ship comes abreast of it; but from the northward it is not discovered so soon. (3:416)

Another example of *which* used as a conjunction may be found in the first passage quoted from Cook, above, and yet another as part of a but-and-which chain below.

4. EXISTENTIAL *here*

In Present-day English, *there* is the only word that commonly introduces "existential" sentences (such as "There are volcanoes on those islands"). In Shakespeare's English, *here* served the same function:

Besides the Animal which I have before mentioned called by the natives *Kangooroo* or *Kanguru* here are Wolves, Possums. (367)	Besides the kanguroo, and the opossum . . . , there are wolves upon this part of the coast. (3:590)
Tame ˙Animals here are none except Dogs. (367)	there are no tame animals here except dogs. (3:591)

5. "MIDDLE" VERB

Verbs in which the active voice has a passive meaning, sometimes called "middle" verbs, were more common in Elizabethan times than they are now. Johnson considered them "a vitious expression" (*Dictionary*, b 2 v).

While this was doing I went a Shore accompany'd by Mr. Banks. (44)	after dinner I went on shore, accompanied by Mr. Banks. (2:43)

Applications

these eat as well or better than spinnage. (367)	these were, in our opinion, not much inferior to spinnage. (3:590)

Johnson's example of this archaism, in the "Grammar" prefixed to the *Dictionary*, is "the grammar is now printing."

6. PREPOSITIONS, PARTICLES

The head ornament projected 5 or 6 feet without the body of the Boat. (283)	The ornament at the head projected five or six feet beyond the body. (3:462)
several of them were naked in the water gathering of Lobsters. (280)	when they went into the water to catch lobsters. (3:456)

7. MISCELLANEOUS EXPRESSIONS, OFTEN EXCISED BY HAWKESWORTH

Double comparative: "they are far more happier than we" (399).

Negative: "they covet not Magnificent Houses" (399).

Proto-progressive: "this one served them . . . to go a fishing in" (397).

Subordinate conjunction: "Notwithstanding we had several interviews . . . yet . . . they never brought" (395).

Intensifier: "I found the Chart tolerable good" (410). "three remarkable large high hills" (315). "prodigious high" (318).

Word order: "him the Gentlemen that had been here before in the Dolphin knew and had often spoke of him as one that . . ." (75).

Datives (?): "I therefore . . . dismiss'd him the quarter deck" (323).

Colloquialisms

1. ASSEVERATION

The Natives do not appear to be numberous neether do they seem to live in large bodies . . . they had not so	they did not appear to be numerous nor to live in societies . . . nor did they touch a single article of all

111

much as touch'd the things
we had left . . . I never saw
the least remains of one.
(312)

that we had left. (3:506)

In a Word they are perhaps
as miserable a set of People
as are this day upon Earth.
(45)

Upon the whole, these
people appeared to be the
most destitute and forlorn,
as well as the most stupid of
human beings. (2:59)

Note in the last quotation from Cook an archaic use of a form of
the existential verb "to be."

No one took the least notice
of her. (102)

No body else seemed willing
to entertain her. (3:151–52)

2. LOOSE SENTENCES

It is indefferently well watered even in the dry
Seasons, with small Brooks
and springs, but no great
Rivers, unless it be in the
wet Season when the low
lands and Vallies near the
Sea I do suppose are mostly
laid under water; the small
brooks may then become
large Rivers but this can
only happen with the Trop-
ick. (393)

it is well watered: we found
innumerable small brooks
and springs, but no great
rivers; these brooks, however, probably become large
in the rainy season. (3:623)

3. INFORMAL DICTION AND VOCABULARY

but it is very probable that
great part of the land is
taken up in Lakes Ponds &c
as is very common in such
like places. (270)

but it is very probable that
the ground, in many places,
is swampy and interspersed
with pools of water. (3:430)

having been already sufficiently harassed with dangers without going to look
for more. (391)

if I had been less harrassed
by danger and fatigue.
(3:619)

4. TOPICALIZATION

With respect to Religion I
beleive these People trouble
themselves very little about
it. (286)

Of the religion of these
people it cannot be sup-
posed that we could learn
much. (3:472)

as to its produce, we must
have been totally ignorant
of [*sic*]. (380)

[Omitted by Hawkesworth.]

5. MISCELLANEOUS EXPRESSIONS, OFTEN OMITTED BY HAWKESWORTH

But-and-which chain:

> However this is of very little concequence to Navigation, I
> only wished to have been certain whether or no it was the
> Southermost land . . . , but the thick Foggy weather, and
> the westerly winds which carried us from the land pre-
> vented me from . . . ; but from X I think it must, and if so
> it must be Cape Horn and lies Y, beeing the mean result of
> Z and which agree'd with those made at A, allowing for B,
> which I found means very accurately to determine. (49)

Idiomatic expressions:

> the night, which promised to be none of the best. (332)
> the needle of which differd from its true posission some
> thing very considerable even above 30 degrees. (331)
> which I have named *Thirsty Sound* by reason we could find
> no fresh water. (332)
> not in such haste but what we might have taken one. (305)

This, the first application of hypotheses developed in chapters 1 and 2, is the most convincing, the most unambiguous, and the easiest to document. Without exception, so far as I know, the genteel John Hawkesworth corrects or omits all solecisms and archaisms and colloquialisms he finds in journals by the lower-middle-class James Cook.

II. *EVELINA*

Like the novels of Fielding and Smollett, Fanny Burney's *Evelina* (1778) is a comic romance, and so it combines characters and sentiments both high (as in classical romance) and low (as in classical comedy). Miss Burney's ear for dialogue was acute, and the number of complicated incorrectnesses spoken by her vulgar sea captain and her petty-bourgeois shopkeepers suggests that she might have had the edicts of prescriptive grammarians in mind. Samuel Johnson had become a fan of hers. He may be counted as one of her most appreciative readers, laughing loudly at the conversation of the shop-keeping Branghtons and committing whole scenes from the novel to memory. But since it was *Evelina* itself that particularly roused Johnson's interest in Fanny Burney, he cannot have had a direct hand in shaping her views on correctness. Born in 1752, Miss Burney was the right age to have assimilated the doctrines of Johnson, Lowth, Kames, and their followers during her formative years. As for the courtly-genteel locutions, they are common currency for both fops and aristocrats in *Evelina*, both true gentlemen and false: courtly-genteel language is a reliable sign of aspirations to upper-class rank, not necessarily an index of true good-breeding.

The vulgar Captain Mirvan enters the novel as Evelina's host in London, father of her best friend, teasing persecutor of her equally vulgar grandmother, Mme. Duval. All his speeches are informal, but the slovenliness of his colloquialisms is nevertheless quite obvious when we compare his language to that of the superlatively genteel Lord Orville (see below):

pr'ythee, friend. (76)

Ay to be sure. (106)

As to them operas. (109)

What, I suppose it is not. (80)

Why, what the D——l, do you come . . .? (80)

Mirvan specializes in the retort discourteous: "No, nor *dish* me nei-ther" is his reply to a Frenchman's query, "*plait-il, Monsieur?*" (119). Asseveration in Mirvan is as homely and just-plain-folks-y as in Moll Flanders:

> wish for nothing so much as . . . (169)
>
> I can see as far into a mill-stone as another man. (120)
>
> glad to know what you can see in e'er a face among them that's worth half a guinea. (107)

Some of Mirvan's grammatical errors are flat-footed:

> what's all that there? (42)
>
> who'd a mind for to keep the young fellows in chace. (59)
>
> them are the first foolish words. (59)
>
> them things. (108)

And some, predictably, can also be classified as archaisms:

> If I ben't mistaken. (108)
>
> Howsomever. (107)
>
> most impertinentest. (136—a double superlative, as in Marc Anthony's "most unkindest cut")
>
> the surprisingest. (167)
>
> you'll be a wanting. (209)
>
> I must e'en tell you. (60)

In note 2, containing dialogue from the first meeting of Captain Mirvan and Mme. Duval, with most of the narrative cropped or summarized, categories of lower-class usage are identified in brackets.[2]

A slightly different set of vulgarities are assigned to the Branghton family of merchants, shopkeepers, cits. Their habits of asseveration, at least those of the girls in the family, are more slangy:

Lord, Polly, only think. (69)

I can't help laughing for my life. (181)

he would not stay with me, all as ever I could say. (202)

monstrous smart. (219)

They run to proverbs, proverbial sayings, and catch phrases:

you're always more ready to spend than to earn. (88)

It's throwing money in the dirt, to pay two coaches for one fare. (88)

thought their singing good enough to serve us for supper. (93)

The first half hour was allotted to *making themselves comfortable*. (68)

In the last phrase quoted, Burney herself is responsible for italics, to mark the actual words used by the Branghtons in this instance; considering what the Branghtons have to do to *make themselves comfortable*, brushing their coats, drying their shoes, and adjusting their headbands for thirty solid minutes, the phrase is surely intended to strike readers as a fussy middle-class euphemism.

Additional lower-class locutions, some of which may claim to be good Elizabethan English:

Now there's Biddy says she thinks nothing of him. (170)

Mr. Smith, as lodges on the first floor. (170)

for that ['because'] he was presently going out. (178)

he saw you and I a-walking up Holborn Hill. (251)

A boy, indeed not such a boy, neither. (174)

It's no fault of mine, I assure you, Miss, only Papa don't like to go. (70)

The Branghtons also favor such middle-class lexical innovations as *grumpy* (168), *funny* (169), and *skimper skamper* (195), none of which are in Johnson's *Dictionary*, all of which have uncertain etymologies and unscholarly provenances.

The contrast between these vulgarisms and the formal gentility of Lord Orville is considerable. Courtly abstractions figure un-

Applications

obtrusively in the polite formulas that make up a good deal of his speech in the early part of the novel (my italics):

> desired to know if I was engaged, or would *honour* him with my hand. (29)
>
> would I *honour* him with my commands to see for her? (31)
>
> Should he have the *pleasure* of bringing me any refreshment? (31)
>
> This lady, Sir, is incapable of *meriting* such an accusation. (33)
>
> talking all the way of the *honour* I had done him. (34)
>
> and lamented that he had not been so fortunate as to hear of it in time to offer his *service*. (71)
>
> This accident, though extremely unfortunate, will not, I hope, be the means of frightening you from *gracing* Ranelagh with your presence in the future? (71)
>
> two persons who I was sensible *merited* not the *honour* of your notice. (240)

Courtly expressions of this sort are common coin with noble and fashionable characters in *Evelina*; they help to make the rake Sir Clement more plausible and Lord Lovell more ridiculous.

But Orville's speech is more truly polite than theirs: he is a "real" gentleman, whose "manners are so elegant, so gentle, so unassuming, that they at once engage esteem, and diffuse complacence" (72). *Gentle, unassuming*, and *complacence* are the key words here: Orville's nobility depends most importantly on his acting and speaking as if he were less noble than his friends, not more—he is the vassal; they are the lords. This is what strikes Evelina about him at first, the "attention and respect" he pays to her despite, or because of, the "foolishness," the "childish" embarrassment of her responses (31–32).

> Far from being indolently satisfied with his own accomplishments, as I have already observed many men here are, tho' without any pretensions to his *merit*, he is most assiduously attentive to *please* and to *serve* all who are in his company. (72; my italics)

The courtier's relation to his lord is here generalized to apply to "all who are in his company." The result is just such a combination of deference and delicacy as has rendered him unpalatable to many twentieth-century readers. He apologizes for inquiring whether Evelina was aware that the two women she was walking arm-in-arm with the previous evening were prostitutes:

> Permit me to assure you that officiousness is not my characteristic, and that I would by no means have risked your displeasure, had I not been fully satisfied you were too generous to be offended, without a real cause of offence.
> (240)

This sentence contains five nouns, and four of them are abstractions (*officiousness, characteristic, displeasure, offense*) with some bearing on the notion of politeness itself. During Evelina's stay at Clifton Hill, Orville "obliges" not only Evelina but also the rest of the company by numerous "attentions," in dramatic contrast to the boorishness of the noble lords who are visiting as well as to the frigid disdain of his well-born sister.

Language in *Evelina*, then, reflects social class, with Captain Mirvan representing the vulgar mob, the Branghtons the petty-bourgeois lower-middle class, Willoughby and Lovell depraved gentility, and Orville true nobility. The fact that social class is not the only variable upon which a given character's speech depends illustrates the difficulty of drawing sociolinguistic conclusions from literary data. But in general our hypotheses seem to hold; lower-class characters speak archaisms, solecisms, and colloquialisms; upper-class characters use courtly-genteel prose.

III. *Tom Jones* and *Clarissa*

Tom Jones and *Clarissa* were both published before linguistic propriety received the detailed public advocacy that it was given by Lowth and Kames and their followers, but doctrines of correctness were in the air. All the early grammar-books pay some lip service to purity of language, and many of them censure one or two individual errors or archaisms. The idea of a British academy which would "correct" and "fix" the language was formally proposed to the Royal Society in the 1660s by Dryden and others, discussed at length by Defoe in his *Essay upon Projects* of 1697, and revived by Swift in a public letter to the Earl of Oxford of 1712, *A Proposal for Correcting, Improving and ascertaining the English Tongue* (see Monroe, 1911). Among Chesterfield's most celebrated letters to his son (written 1748–49 though not published until 1774) are a number that denigrate "vulgar, low expressions," proverbs, slang, and "homely, coarse" language. "Any one barbarism, solecism, or vulgarism" in a formal letter, he advises, will reverberate "to your disgrace and ridicule" (4:1380, 1407, 1442, 1443).

It is therefore understandable that relations between syntax and social class are less consistent in Fielding and Richardson than in Hawkesworth and Burney. The association of courtly-genteel language with selected noble lords and of solecisms, archaisms, and colloquialisms with low, comic, working-class characters does hold true for both these earlier novelists, but the speeches of genteel characters in Fielding and Richardson are by no means free of these lower-class linguistic features. We can detect something similar to the same differentiation between lower-class language and lower-middle-class (bourgeois) language in Richardson as in Burney. Although Richardson and Fielding had different feelings about the aristocracy as such, they seem to agree to put courtly-genteel expressions in the mouths both of vicious upper-class libertines and of true gentlefolk.

Fielding uses courtly-genteel prose to negotiate within quasi-feudal forms of patronage and dependency, in petitions and polite letters, in discussions of courtship, dueling, and parental authority. Early in the story, Tom has "a *Favour* to ask" of Sophia, "which he hoped her *Goodness* would comply with," namely to "sollicit [*sic*] her *Interest* on Behalf of" the Seagrim Family (1:167–68; bk. 4, ch. 5). And when Harriet Fitzpatrick attempts a reconciliation with the Westerns, she writes a letter expressing her earnest wishes that

> the Care which I have shown on this Occasion for the Good of my Family, will recommend me again to the *Favour* of a Lady who hath always exerted so much Zeal for the *Honour* and true *Interest* of us all. (2:804; bk. 15, ch. 6)

This is both a formal petition and a polite letter; so are Tom's specious proposals of marriage to Lady Bellaston, in which he prates of "the *Honour* of your Ladyship's Commands," the "*Favours*" she has conferred on him, the "*Obligations*" pecuniary and otherwise that he has received "at your Hands" (2:820–21; bk. 15, ch. 9).

One vicious courtship in *Tom Jones* is couched in courtly-genteel prose, as is one virtuous one. Having begun his wooing of Sophia by trying to rape her, Lord Fellamar protests in a formal visit that he has "no Thoughts but what are directed to your *Honour* and *Interest*." Sophia answers that "If your Lordship will *merit* my Gratitude, there is but one Way." This piece of politeness produces, as if automatically, a courtly compliment to the effect that everything and anything Fellamar can perform "is so much your *due*" that it does not call for ('deserve') gratitude. Fielding as narrator acknowledges that Fellamar's courtly conversation contains "much which we do not perfectly understand, and perhaps it could not all be strictly reconciled either to Sense or Grammar" (2:902–3; bk. 17, ch. 8).

Nevertheless, when Tom and Sophia are finally reunited, free to express their real feelings for each other after all those banishments, taboos, and misunderstandings, the reconcilement is conducted partly in courtly-genteel terms. It is the "*Displeasure*" of a feudal lord (or lady, in the person of his beloved) that Tom has incurred, and Sophia reminds him that "you best know whether you have *deserved*" that displeasure.

> 'Indeed, Madam,' answered he, 'you yourself are as well apprized of all my *Demerits*.'

Sophia's father, having bullied her into consenting to be married the next day, breaks the news to Allworthy, whose reaction is perfectly genteel:

> 'I hope, Madam, my Nephew will *merit* so much *Goodness*, and will be always as sensible as myself of the great *Honour* you have done my Family.'

Sophia refuses to repent "of any Promise in *Favour* of Mr. Jones," and Allworthy reassures her that she is betrothed to "one who will be sensible of your great *Merit*, and who will at least use his best Endeavours to *deserve* it" (2:971, 975–76; bk. 18, ch. 12).

Courtly language is one thing, in Fielding's mind, courtly values quite another. Sophia's vain, silly, treacherous maid is not given the name "Honour" for nothing. Young Nightingale remarks sarcastically on the cheapness of Lady Bellaston's "*Favours*," with the result that Tom promptly decides on "turning himself out of her *Service*" (2:819; bk. 15, ch. 9: Fielding's italics). As linguistic evidence of Jenny Jones's "extraordinary Parts ['abilities'] and Improvements," she has an elegant, courtly-genteel speech of thanks to say in book 1 (54), but that does not prevent her from becoming the mistress of a villainous soldier in book 9. For all his proletarian name, Tom Jones has enough of the heroic in him to believe that it was "as much incumbent on him to accept a Challenge to Love, as if it had been a Challenge to Fight" (2:715; bk. 13, ch. 7), but it is just this courtly trait that gets him into the worst trouble with Sophia.

After all, Fielding believes, "the highest Life is much the dullest, and affords very little Humour or Entertainment"; it is the "lower Spheres" that furnish opportunities not only for nonstandard characters but also for nonstandard language (2:743; bk. 14, ch. 1). Most of Fielding's working-class people lapse at some point into archaic colloquialisms, though not consistently. Mrs. Partridge, quite a minor character in the novel as a whole, has a long, ludicrous lament to address to Allworthy in book 2, with malapropisms marked in italics and colorful colloquialisms, plus a handful of archaisms, though no solecisms to take notice of:

> He hath injured my Bed many's the good time and often . . . if he had not broke . . . Yes, you Villain, you have defiled my own Bed, you have [cf. Liza Dolittle, 'I'm a good girl, I am'] . . . I have Marks enow about my Body. (1:99–101; bk. 2, ch. 6)

The Seagrim women vent their envy in archaisms, dialectal pronunciations, solecisms, and catch phrases:

> You think yourself more handsomer than any of us. . . . You'd better have minded what the Parson says, and not a harkened after Men Voke. . . . and what was the mighty Matter of that? . . . You shan't want Money neither . . . thof I was obliged . . . above all them Things . . . Marry come up . . . Some Voke walked a-voot. (1:184–85; bk. 4, ch. 9)

Black George is almost equally unrefined in speech (2:918; bk. 10, ch. 2), and Honour has her own distinctive lower-class linguistic habits: "I speaks no Scandal"; "I never was a dremd of any such Thing"; "because as why"; "who dares for to offer to presume for to say" (2:746 and 825, 1:208, 2:604; bk. 14, ch. 2, bk. 15, ch. 10, bk. 4, ch. 14, bk. 11, ch. 8). That last phrase is a characteristic bit of pseudogentility ('dares to offer to presume to say'), strapped together with old-fashioned infinitives ("*for* to offer . . . *for* to say").

Dialectal locutions are often a sign of lower-class status in the eighteenth century for many of the same reasons that archaisms are: they indicate in every case some distance from courtly and urban standards of culture and refinement. Dialectal usage quite often *is* archaic, since in the eighteenth century old forms and structures tended to persist in more isolated areas. (Exceptions to this rule found in semi-rural communities of twentieth-century Norway and India seem not to have bearing on eighteenth-century Britain; see Gumperz, 10 and 38.)

The question of how closely a given character's dialect correlates with his or her social class is complicated by a comic tradition within which dialect speakers may belong to any class at all. Comic Irish noblemen are among the earliest stage figures to speak in dialect, and their descendants populate the novel from 1749 (see Duggan, 1937). There is always something disreputable about them, however, as there is about Squire Western, for all his great estate and magistrate's prerogatives. In the case of comic aristocrats, as in the case of real-life booby squires, syntax and social class do not match.

Fielding went to some trouble, however, to put dialect into the mouths of several of his lowlife characters. In addition to the Seagrim family, as cited above, we have Fitzpatrick in book 10 with his *upon my Shoul* and *you have bate* ['beaten'] *me* (2:528, 530; bk. 10, ch. 2). Squire Western's west-country dialect seems to thicken and curdle when he has been talking to polite or courtly people: "And to gu, . . . to zet *Allworthy* against thee vor it.—D——n un, if the Parson had unt had his Petticuoats on. . . ." "Wout unt persuade me canst not ride in a Coach, wouldst?" (1:219; bk. 5, ch. 2, and 2:801; bk. 15, ch. 5). At least twice in the novel Fielding puts dialect words in italics (1:378–79; bk. 7, ch. 13, and 1:305; bk. 6, ch. 10). Many of the quaint misspellings of Honour's letter to Tom can be explained as phonetic transcriptions of Somersetshire dialect, "hur

Lashipp," "Uman" ('Woman'), "gud" ('good'), "Sarvis," and "sartenly" (2:825; bk. 15, ch. 10).

Fielding, in sum, exploits the stylistics of social class to add vivid color to the human comedy of *Tom Jones*. We can be fairly sure, however, that he was not as conscious of these relations as Fanny Burney was, because most of his genteel characters are occasionally guilty of archaisms and solecisms—and so is the narrator himself. Fielding learned to speak and write forty years before the age of Johnson and Lowth.

And so Lady Bellaston says "you was" (2:817; bk. 15, ch. 9), and Tom says "honestest" (2:754; bk. 14, ch. 4); Tom uses *without* as a subordinate conjunction in a polite letter (2:820; bk. 15, ch. 9), and Allworthy opens a harangue with "Look'ee" (as does Tom) (1:70; bk. 1, ch. 12, and 2:755; bk. 14, ch. 4). I give additional examples in note 3. Interestingly, the one person whose English is always pure and not *too* courtly is Sophia.[3]

The case of Samuel Richardson is similar, with variations. Like Fielding, Richardson's gentlefolk speak courtly-genteel phrases, and write them, but technical terms of courtly-genteel prose play a more prominent role in *Clarissa* than in *Tom Jones* because it is so much more focused on courtship and the heavy-handed, patriarchal dependencies of the Harlowe family. Also, since Clarissa herself is put on display as a model of gentility, her language exemplifies certain (middle-class) ideals of (upper-class) elegance. The occasional ill-bred servant or rustic clown in *Clarissa* speaks the lower-class English that our hypothesis predicts, perhaps a more literary version of it than in *Tom Jones*. One or two aristocrats are shown to have bourgeois souls by the bourgeois language they use.

Clarissa's predicament at the beginning of the novel seems to have been conceived in terms of courtly systems of dependency and appeal. Her grandfather changed his *will* in Clarissa's *favor* because she had always been "a matchless young creature in her *duty* to me" (1:21). This extraordinary *indulgence* increases her brother's and sister's resentment "of my two uncles' *favour* for me, and of the *pleasure* I had given my father and them by this act of *duty*" (1:55). At the beginning of the book, however, she still "has *interest* enough to disengage" herself from two unwanted suitors (1:19). Clarissa, in other words, is vassal to the older generation's lordships, and it is her refusal to count betrothal to the vulgar Roger Solmes as a valid *duty* that cancels all her *merits* in their eyes.

Courtly-genteel terminology plays a key role in the early confrontations between Clarissa and her family.

> My father . . . told me, that I had met with too much *indulgence* in being allowed to refuse this gentleman, and the other gentleman; and it was now his turn to be obeyed.
>
> Very true, my mother said, and hoped his *will* would not now be disputed by a child so *favoured*.
>
> To show they were all of a sentiment, my Uncle Harlowe said he hoped his beloved niece only wanted to know her father's *will* to obey it.
>
> And my Uncle Antony, in his rougher manner, added that surely I would not give them reason to apprehend that I thought my grandfather's *favour* to me had made me independent of them all. (1:30)

A few pages later, Clarissa struggles to maintain her role as a dutiful daughter:

> [Clarissa:] I have never yet opposed your *will*—
>
> [Her father:] . . . Don't let me run the fate of all who show *indulgence* to your sex . . .
>
> [Clarissa, "going to make protestations of *duty*":] Good sir, be *pleased* to hear me. My brother and my sister, I fear—
>
> [Her father:] Your brother and sister shall not be spoken against, girl. They have a just concern for the *honour* of my family.
>
> [Clarissa:] And I hope, sir—
>
> [Her father:] Hope nothing. Tell me not of hopes, but of facts. I ask nothing of you but what is in your power to comply with, and what it is your *duty* to comply with.
>
> [Clarissa:] Then, sir, I will comply with it; but yet I hope from your *goodness*— (1:36–37)

There are three more *duty*'s, two more *will*'s, a *pleasure*, and a *disfavour* on page 37 of the Everyman edition. Every party to these last dialogues—hard-fought battles in Clarissa's war of resistance—justifies him- or herself in terms of courtly abstractions.

Applications

Richardson tells us in his "Author's Preface" (1759) that Clarissa's letters exhibit not only "the noblest principles of virtue and religion" but also a supreme "delicacy of sentiments": she is presented to us as a model of upper-class refinement. We may suppose that if there are any stylistic features that embodied for Richardson the highest ideals of genteel or elegant language, he will have incorporated them into Clarissa's letters, especially the early ones that antedate her intolerable persecutions at Mrs. Sinclair's house.

Courtly motives in Clarissa's letters are often specified in a main verb, downgrading actions to infinitive complements. We can see how polite this syntactic structure is by comparing a plain action, in the left-hand column following, with what Richardson wrote, in the right:

Lovelace on the fourth day inquired in person	he *thought fit* on the fourth day to make in person the same inquiries. (1:19)
My father hopes you to be all obedience	[my] father . . . *is willing* to hope you to be all obedience. (1:34)
My father hinted to Mr. Lovelace that	My father *was pleased* to hint to Mr. Lovelace that. (1:18)
My mother told me	[My mother] *was so good* as to tell me. (1:87)
You will write frequently I	What a generosity *will it be* in you, to write as frequently from friendship as I. (1:77)

Duty and *honor* are of course primary motives and attributes in the world of the courtier; Clarissa's predicament is that different versions of these ideals have come directly in conflict with each other. Clarissa really does want to obey her parents, but cannot: "how difficult is it, my dear [she writes to Anna], to give a negative where both *duty* and inclination join to make one wish to *oblige*" (1:32).

A second characteristic feature of Clarissa's most elegant letters is the frequency with which abstractions (not people) function as agents. "My *duty* will not permit me so far to suppose my father arbitrary as to make a plea of that arbitrariness to you" (1:79), she tells her mother; it is not she, Clarissa, who will or will not "suppose," but her "duty."

my spirit would not permit me to be *obliged*. (2:75)

his insolence shall never make me discover a weakness unworthy of a person distinguished by your friendship. (2:45)

Ought I to widen my error by obstinacy and resentment . . . ? (2:9)

and hope that my sincerity . . . will atone. (2:48)

The courtier displays his craft of courtesy most conspicuously in ceremonies, not in practical conversation; and some of Clarissa's most spectacular courtly locutions occur when she is ceremoniously pledging her service to someone or bowing herself out of the presence of the friend whose humble servant she so elaborately claims to be—that is, in the subscriptions of letters. On one occasion Clarissa fears that she has written too "freely" of her immediate family, so she confides in Anna's "discretion,"

> that you will avoid reading to or transcribing for others, such passages as may have the appearance of treating too freely the parental, or even the fraternal character, or induce others to censure for a supposed failure in duty to the one, or decency to the other,
> Your truly affectionate,
> C. Harlowe.
>
> (1:62)

The art of courtly subscription consists partly in concealing art, in bowing oneself out of the room without drawing attention; therefore, the conventional identification of oneself as a "humble, obedient servant" or "dutiful daughter" is incorporated into a final sentence that has a different purpose. In this case Clarissa has complimented Anna's "discretion" (an abstraction) by detailing what it will do or not do; it will not transcribe passages that might induce "others" to censure her truly affectionate friend, Clarissa. The four antitheses woven into this sentence enhance its elaborateness and elegance.

Courtly-genteel language plays a role in defining the full dimensions of Lovelace's wickedness. Unambiguously aristocratic as he is by birth, schooled from his youth in modern languages and the classics, Lovelace nevertheless cannot break free of his own rakishness; since to be a rake, for Richardson, is to have abandoned basic moral and social principles of value, and given certain Shaftes-burian assumptions on the interdependence of goodness and beauty (elegance), Lovelace is never at home in the courtly-genteel mode. A truly polite person, like Clarissa herself, is committed to those social principles that determine what *duties* and *merits* truly deserve *honor*. Lovelace hasn't the least concern for such matters, only for his own ego. As a rake he subscribes to a number of anti-social doctrines; his real inner life (as opposed to his hypocritical or plotting life) is that of an outcast from society. Therefore, when he does use courtly-genteel style it is merely as a ticket to plausibility, as a mask.

The everyday, utilitarian uses of courtly-genteel terms, how-ever, are hard even for Lovelace to avoid. Trying to deprecate Cla-rissa's submissiveness to her parents, he talks about "your high notions of a *duty* that can never be *deserved* where you place it" (2:204). He speaks of "my earnestness to procure her to *favour* my friends with her company" (2:240), and promises that "the best bed . . . should be at her *service*" (2:241). "Had she *honoured* us with more of her conversation, she would have been less disgusted with ours" (2:239), writes Lovelace to Belford. These last three quota-tions are all from a single letter devoted to the dinner-party when Lovelace's cronies—Mowbrey, Tourville, and company—get their first sight of Clarissa; since Lovelace is narrating a human trans-action in which courtesy plays a central role, small wonder that courtly-genteel terminology makes its appearance, however briefly and unobtrusively.

When Lovelace is trying to be polite (which does not happen very often), he draws on a limited but undeniably courtly repertory of phrases. "I hope, Madam," he says to Clarissa upon finding her dressed to go out, "I shall have the *honour* to attend you" (2:220). In one of his beseeching moods he tells Clarissa that "you have re-ceived with *favour* my addresses; you have made me hope for the *honour* of your consenting hand" (2:196). At one point, having suc-ceeded in putting his arms around Clarissa's waist, "the dear crea-ture so absent that she knew not the *honour*" she permitted him, he claims to be "the most *obliged* of men" (2:141).

Several of the more elaborate courtly locutions in Lovelace's letters, however, are hypocritical. We know that he dislikes the vir-tuous and discerning Mrs. Norton, of whom he writes, fraudu-lently, "Mrs. Norton is so good a women, that I shall think she lays me under an *obligation* if she will put it in my power to *serve* her" (2:93). Lying in his teeth, he assures Clarissa that she shall be her own mistress: "nor will I ask for your *favour* but as upon full proof I shall appear to *deserve* it (1:482). After all, as Clarissa points out at the start, Lovelace "is far from being a polite man" (1:357). Belford acknowledges that Lovelace's honor is "false *honour*" (3:466). "There is nothing . . . more delightful," writes Lovelace in the heat of the chase, "than for lovers to be conferring and receiving *obligations* from each other" (2:67), which sententious saying he goes on to illustrate with a heavily sexual barnyard fable of strutting cocks and "half-willing" hens.

A good way of demonstrating the speciousness of Lovelace's gentility is to compare his habitual bantering style, or even the routine insincerities of his attempts to be polite, with a characteristic speech in *Sir Charles Grandison*. Three hundred pages into the first volume of that novel, when Harriet Byron could reasonably be supposed to have recovered from the stresses and strains of her abduction by Sir Hargrove, Sir Charles brings his second sister to call on her. Harriet is still self-conscious about owing such extraordinary "obligations" to such a man as Sir Charles, and blushes deeply. Sir Charles takes her by the hand, leads her to the window, and speaks,

> My sister Charlotte, madam, was impatient to present to you her beloved sister. Lady L. was as impatient to attend you. My Lord L. was equally desirous to claim the *honour* of your acquaintance. They insisted upon my introducing my Lord. I thought it was too precipitant a visit, and might hurt your delicacy, and make Charlotte and me appear, as if we had been ostentatiously boasting of the opportunities that had been thrown into our hands, to do a very common *service*. I think I see that you are hurt. Forgive me, madam, I will follow my own judgment another time. Only be assured of this, that your *merits*, and not the *service*, have drawn this visit upon you.
>
> I could not be displeased at this polite address, as it helped me to an excuse for behaving so like a fool, as he might think, since he knew not the cause.
>
> You are very *obliging*, Sir. My Lord and Lady L. do me great *honour*. Miss Grandison cannot do any-thing but what is agreeable to me. In such company, I am but a common person: But my gratitude will never let me look upon

your seasonable protection as a common *service*. I am only
anxious for the consequences to yourself. (1:312–13)

This exchange is governed by the same conventions of polite friendship that obtained in letters by Thomas More and Pope, quoted
above on page 83: each party protests that his *services* are no more
than are *deserved*, but that the *favour* and *honour* the other party has
conferred on him far exceed his *merits*. None of Lovelace's letters
makes any attempt to be polite in this courtly way.

At the opposite extreme from Clarissa's letters are the letters
and speeches of a cluster of servants and country folk, "Rosebud,"
Betty Barnes, Joseph Leman, Will Summers, Hannah Burton, and
an unnamed tenant belonging to Anna Howe who serves as mes-
senger; all such characters indulge in colloquialisms, solecisms, and
archaisms to one degree or another.

> her father cannot give her but a few things. (1:172)
>
> I have heard famous scholars often and often say. (1:319)
>
> to let your Honner knoe as how I have been emploied.
> (2:143)
>
> who is of late com'd out. (2:143)
>
> I knowed I dursted not look. (3:21)
>
> which has made me quite and clene helpless. (3:326)
>
> for the beef was woundily corned. (3:161)

Some of these expressions sound as if they had been made up with
a grammar rule in mind rather than overheard in street or field. As
in Burney and Swift, proverbs and catch phrases in Richardson are
the sign of a bourgeois mentality, whether in a doting peer (Lord
M., 3:322) or in a pert maidservant (Betty Barnes, 1:320).

Where the relations between syntax and social class are less
clear is in archaic usages by Lovelace, Clarissa, and other genteel
characters, some of which seem deliberately chosen by Richardson
for atmospheric or stylistic purposes, others not. Lovelace affects
"the Roman style" (I, 144; Richardson's note) in his letters to Belford; that is, he addresses his close friends in the second person
singular, *thee* and *thou*. This usage would appear to be an archaism,
probably associated with conscious imitation of the gallantries of
chivalric romance (S. Baker, 1964). Lowth censures it as "disused"
(48), and its replacement by second person plurals was under way

in English and all the major European languages at this time (Brown and Gilman, 1960). But Clarissa herself modulates from the more formal *you* to the familiar *thou* in the middle of a dialogue with Betty Barnes, as an expression of disdain not unlike the *thou*-ing Sir Toby Belch recommends to Sir Andrew Aguecheek (1:321; *Twelfth Night*, III, ii, 45).

Deliberate archaisms may be intended to advertise Lovelace's affinities with the stereotypical Restoration rake. Just as his favorite poets are Waller, Otway, and Cowley, so among his favorite epithets are a number of seventeenth-century words, *varlet*, *arrant*, *wot*, *prate*, *methinks*, *Zounds*, *plaguy*. On the other hand, not Lovelace alone but Clarissa and Anna as well employ Elizabethan negatives and imperatives: "they succeeded not" (1:16); "nor upbraid thou me" (3:177). The fruity, quasi-heroic attitudes that Richardson endows Clarissa and Lovelace with are compatible with old-fashioned word order: "Nor let your generous heart be moved" (3:16); "this my intrepidity" (3:43). *Had-had* conditionals contribute to the same faintly antique syntactic climate: "I had still held this resolution . . . , had not the two passed days furnished . . ." (3:2).[4]

Enough traces of less poetic archaisms remain in the letters of genteel characters, however, to weaken blanket generalizations about language and social class in *Clarissa*, archaisms that would be proscribed by the grammarians of the next decades as solecisms. Clarissa herself writes "you was pleased" (1:167), and "mighty prudent" (1:266), and "except I am to be refuged" (1:323). *For that* appears as a subordinate conjunction not only in Lovelace (3:93) but also in the summary of the contents of individual letters added to the 1751 edition by the editor, Richardson himself (1:523). Although these are small points thinly scattered among the many myriads of words of this large novel, they confirm a hypothesis that standards for correct usage were not well established before the 1760s.[5]

IV. HUMPHRY CLINKER

A brief examination of the way linguistic usage and social class do—and do not—correlate in Tobias Smollett's last, best novel, *Humphry Clinker* (1771), will illustrate some of the problems of applying the generalizations so far developed to actual texts. Selective quotation can supply evidence that most of Smollett's genteel characters use courtly language at appropriate moments, and all his

Applications

common folk use "lower-class" language, in several delicious varieties. It is possible to sift out just enough distinctive traits in the language of each major letter-writer to make a case that each has his or her own style. But there isn't one well-born personage in *Humphry Clinker* who does not draw on archaic or incorrect locutions at one time or another. Moreover, extensive passages in letters by the two principal correspondents of the book, Jery Melford and Matt Bramble, are written in a single narrative style with a voice that has almost no interest in either courtly or lower-class usage. Those two characters are thereby stylistically limited and play some of the roles of a "narrator-in-general."

In fact there is less courtly-genteel language in *Humphry Clinker* than might be expected, given Jery Melford's obsession with "the privilege of a gentleman" (8) and Matt Bramble's fear of "nothing so much as dishonour" (28). Jery insists on his rank as a member of the gentry. What most disturbs him about his sister's suitor Wilson is the common birth that he ascribes to any such member of a company of strolling actors. Jery seems to be ready to challenge almost anyone to a duel on almost pretext or excuse, and joins willingly in the "sport" of his aristocratic friends at Oxford. Matt is of course the pattern of a good country squire and therefore by right a gentleman. Like Jery, he is inflammable and offers to fight a West Indian colonel at the first sign of disrespect. There seems to be a clear line drawn in Smollett's novel between the gentry (Matt, Jery, Lydia, and various land-owning minor characters) and ungenteel lower-class types such as Win Jenkins and Humphry himself.

"The reputation of an intrigue" with a woman-about-town, writes Jery, "does me no *honour* at all" (59). "If this trifle can be of any *service* to you," says Matt, as he hands a twenty-pound note to a destitute widow, "I beg you will accept it" (21). The only being on whom Tabitha bestows any affection is her dog Chowder; "one would imagine," writes Jery, that "she had distinguished this beast with her *favour* on account of his ugliness and ill-nature" (62). A chance encounter between Matt and a certain Mr. Serle starts inauspiciously: "Sir, I have not the *honour* to know you. . . . The person you are *pleased* to treat so cavalierly, is a gentleman of some consequence"; but when Serle recognizes Bramble as an old acquaintance, he pulls off his spectacles and acknowledges "in a mitigated tone, 'Surely I am much *obliged*—'" (68). Lydia mentions "the paths of *honour* and virtue" (11), and prudently declines "the *favour* of a salute" (9). A gentleman-clergyman later in the book repudiates all "reflections upon my order, the *honour* of which I think my-self in *duty* bound to maintain," hinting that despite his cloth he is quite willing to fight a duel if sufficiently provoked (74).

Such expressions, and a few more (76, 112–13, 142–44), may be read as the common coin of well-bred social intercourse in the second half of the eighteenth century. They fall far short of the convoluted politenesses that adorn the lips or pen of Clarissa or Lord Orville. They seem almost completely cut off from the courtly relationships and refined codes of behavior from which they derive. So it does not surprise us to find some of the same locutions in the comic Irish adventurer Mackilligut: "I never had the *honour* to sea [*sic*] your face before," says he with ironical politeness to Matt. "Your humble *servant*, good sir . . . I'm come . . . to offer my best *services* to you . . . You must know I am to have the *honour* to open a ball next door to-morrow" (30). Humphry himself has picked up some courly-genteel tag phrases to use in flattering Tabitha: "May it *please* your ladyship's worship . . . all for the love and pleasure of *serving* such an excellent lady" (84).

Most of what Humphry has to say faithfully reflects his lower-class rural origin (not his genteel paternity). "I am so, an please your worthy ladyship" (81), says he to Tabitha, using the late Middle English subordinate conjunction *an* ('if'). "I'll engage to ge'en a good drubbing, that, may hap, will do'en service" (209–10). "I won't turn my back on e'er a he in the county of Wilts" (83). These last two show an overlapping provenance in dialectal and archaic usages in lower-class eighteenth-century English. There are some signs, however, that when Humphry is "matthewmurphy'd into a fine young gentleman" (337), that is, discovered to be Matt Bramble's illegitimate son, his speech changes: the argument he is reported to make for honoring his informal engagement to Win Jenkins, when translated from indirect to direct discourse, has a solid upper-middle-class feel to it: 'I own I have a kindness for the young woman, and have reason to think she looks upon me with a favourable eye; I consider this mutual manifestation of good will, as an engagement understood, which ought to be binding to the conscience of an honest man; and I hope the 'squire and you will be of the same opinion, when you shall be at leisure to bestow any thought about the matter' (334).

Not only are the letters of Matt Bramble deficient in courtly posturing, they have also their share of inelegant constructions, small archaisms, minor colloquialisms, and solecisms—not in great abundance, but enough to give substance and verisimilitude to his role as old-fashioned country squire. "I an't married to Tabby," he exclaims, and to this dialectal or archaic negative auxiliary he adds an old-fashioned subject-auxiliary inversion, "nor did I beget the other two" (12). He uses the familiar second person *thou* to Humphry (84), and the obsolescent third person *hath* (36). "Methinks I hear you," writes Matthew, and "forsooth! . . . 'sdeath" (34, 12). "I should be glad to know what kind of powders you was distributing" (100). The speech community to which Matt belongs is not yet self-conscious about English subjunctives: "If my friend Sir Thomas was a single man," he writes to Dr. Lewis, "I would not trust such a handsome wench in his family" (38); Lowth, Campbell, and their followers prescribe the subjunctive for contrary-to-fact conditions like this. In Bath he observes "springs . . . gushing spontaneous on every side" (46); in Clifton he overhears someone "talking very loud and vehement" (13); Lowth would have preferred the adverbial form here. In the old days, says Matt, "the substantial tradesman wont ['was accustomed'] to pass his evenings at the alehouse for fourpence half-penny" (88).

Jery's case is similar but less marked. His letters, addressed to "Sir Watkin Phillips, Bart.," resort occasionally to such informalities as "set out a horseback" (282) or "burst out a-laughing" (20), and lapse occasionally into incorrectnesses such as "he was scarce warm in the lodgings when . . ." (28), or "having tore" (80), "who had drove" (82). The predominant style in both Jery's and Matt's letters, however, is concatenated, jocular, and nominal. Perhaps this is the habitual narrative style of *Humphry Clinker* as a whole, and it seems either unrelated to social class or, broadly speaking, middle class in origin and tenor—neither courtly nor vulgar, but a little over-educated, stuffy, garrulous.

"Concatenated": long sentences made of numerous independent and subordinate clauses, all correctly but sometimes redundantly linked by conjunctions and conjunctive adverbs; a fondness for ending or stringing out sentences with relative clauses. "Nominal": deverbal nouns (nouns derived from verbs: see Marchand, 303) in preference to finite verbs; frequent use of the stative verbs *have* and *be* as finite verbs; abstractions as agents; "light verbs" (*have, take, make, do*) plus deverbal nouns (see Live); lots of gerunds and infinitives. For example:

If I did not know that [conjunction] the exercise [deverbal] of your profession [deverbal] has habituated you to the hearing [gerund] of complaints [deverbal], I should make [light verb] a conscience of troubling [gerund] you with my correspondence [deverbal], which [relative] may be truly called The lamentation [deverbal] of Matt Bramble. Yet [conjunction] I cannot help thinking [gerund], I have [stative] some right [abstraction] to discharge [infinitive] the overflowings [gerund] of my spleen upon you, whose [relative] province [abstraction] it is [stative] to remove [infinitive] those disorders [abstraction] that [relative] occasioned it; and [conjunction] let me tell you, it is [stative] no small alleviation [deverbal] of my grievances [deverbal], that [conjunction] I have [stative] a sensible friend, to whom [relative] I can communicate my crusty humours, which [relative], by retention [deverbal], would grow intolerably acrimonious. (33)

It is in Win Jenkins that Smollett's mastery of the stylistics of lower-class comic English is most brilliant, most obvious, and most risible. She is a gifted malapropist, who mangles the conventions of correct usage, grammar, and spelling with such tremendous éclat and brazen unconcern that her letters became a linguistic saturnalia, defying linguistic authority and setting us free from mere coherence and common sense. Win writes "mare" for *mayor*, "cunty" for *county*, "grease" for *grace*, "suppurate" for *separate*, "Smuck" for *smock*, "farting" for *farthing*, and "tail-baring" for *tale-bearing* (Boggs; S. Baker, 1961).

Tabitha, almost Win's equal in gross, hilarious, sexual-physical blunders, writes "jowls" for *jewels*, "bumdaffee" for *Daffy's Elixir* (a laxative), "rumping" for *romping*, "shit" for *shirt*, "accunt" for *account*. We can, however, distinguish between the lower-class English that comes naturally to Win and the uneducated philistinism of Tabitha. Miss Bramble is of gentle blood but apparently never bothered to acquire much education or general culture (contrast the sententious literary romanticism of letters by her niece Lydia). The socially degrading effect of parsimony is felt in Tabitha's lower-middle-class use of catch phrases and proverbial sayings: "a fool and his money [are] soon parted" (83); "that's another good penny out of my pocket" (44). In spite of her rank in the social hierarchy, her letters are sprinkled with archaic constructions, colloquialisms, solecisms, and some dialectal (or merely rural?) usages: "the maids . . . may be sat a spinning" (6); "Let me know if Alderney's calf be sould yet, and what he fought ['fetched']" (6); "An't he game?" (53); "You was called" (192); "the cock crowed so natural" (53); "Howsomever" (45); "unsartain" (45); "skim ['scum'] of the hearth ['earth']" (78); "mought" (78); "would you go for to offer, for to arguefy me out of my senses?" (22); "ne'er a pig in the parish shall thrust his snout in it, with my good-will" (78).

In Win's case, rural pronunciations, colloquialisms (especially catch phrases), solecisms, and archaisms are so common as to be almost the rule rather than the exception. Her first letter, 285 words long, includes the following:

> hoping to hear the same; and that you . . . (nonparallel construction)
>
> We have been all in a sad taking. (misplaced quantifier? plus catch phrase)
>
> Miss Liddy had like to have run away. (archaic?)
>
> young master and he would adone themselves a mischief. (colloquial)
>
> no more I shall. (colloquial asseveration)
>
> we servints should see all and say nothing. (proverbial)
>
> Chowder has had . . . and came. (non-parallel construction)
>
> in a terrible pickle. (slang)
>
> I do suppose. (archaic)
>
> madam Gwyllim will be a prying. (archaic)
>
> an ould coat. (rural pronunciation)
>
> John says as how tis. (colloquial or archaic)
>
> parquisites . . . sartain. (rural pronunciation) (7)

There's plenty more of this in subsequent letters: "that's not his name neither," "thof he acted," "na'r a smoak ['smock'] upon our backs," "no thoughts either of wan or t'other" (42–43). Large portions of Win's more enthusiastic effusions are overconcatenated into but-and-which chains: 'She has tould A, and disclosed B for Mr. Wilson, and that's not his name, and thof he acted C, he is D, and she has gi'en me E, which Mrs. Drab says F . . .' (42). We classified

this trait as a colloquialism in Moll Flanders, and it is certainly that
in Win Jenkins, though it is also something more, an expression of
character: self-interested garrulity, the heady effervescence of a
babbling Welsh brook.

Humphry Clinker, then, seems to conform in general outline to
the hypotheses for relationships between language and social class
that were postulated in chapters 1 and 2, with notable exceptions.
Courtly-genteel terminology is less common than might be expected on the basis of Jery's bristly self-consciousness about his own
rank. It makes a perfunctory appearance in the mouths of Mackilligut and Humphry as they pay court to their betters, and it crops up
in the language of polite conversation among strangers and in the
context of dueling, but it has no substantial role to play in defining
character or predicament, or in expressing complex attitudes, as it
does in Richardson. The bottom end of the social hierarchy is
where Smollett's comic genius has full stylistic play. In Win Jenkins's
letters, the archaisms and rural colloquialisms of lower-class speech
are a perfect "ground" for the "figure" delineated by her celebrated malapropisms, her inspired lexical ineptitude. To appreciate how nearly essential lower-class usage is to the full voltage of
Win's personality, compare Mrs. Malaprop herself, from Richard
Sheridan's contemporaneous play, *The Rivals* (1775). The main fabric of Mrs. Malaprop's speech is educated upper-middle-class English, and the lexical blunders stitched into that fabric at intervals
are pedantic not vulgar, over-educated not under-educated.

> I would by no means wish a daughter of mine to be a pro-
> geny ['prodigy'] of learning.
>
> Then, Sir, she should have a supercilious ['superficial']
> knowledge in accounts.
>
> I would have her instructed in geometry ['geography'],
> that she might know something of the contagious ['con-
> tiguous'] countries.
>
> I hope you will represent her to the Captain as an object
> not altogether illegible ['ineligible']. (421)

Like Win, Mrs. Malaprop has personality to be reckoned with;
but its domain is the drawing room, its nourishment the self-love of
a middle-aged woman who would like nothing better than to be

thought of as demirep. Lower-class language is what places Win in the pantry, not the parlor, and detoxifies her vanity. The citified airs and vapors, the "asterisks" and exclamations of a lass whose speech shows her to be as rural and common as a cow path or a country lane, can't do as much harm as the same pretensions in a respectable lady.

V. Bows and Curtsies: Courtly Letters

Courtly-genteel prose is aesthetically neutral, neither ugly nor beautiful in itself. In the hands of a skilled writer it can serve the purposes of high verbal artistry; in the hands of a bungler it can be as ill-shaped as any other prose. Here is a sample from the unpleasing end of the spectrum:

> Sir, / Though I give you very humble thanks for the honour of your remembrance, yet I shall always remain indebted to you, as making more account of the least of your favours, than all the respects I am able to render you. Continue only in obliging me of that fashion (though I be entirely yours already) and believe (if you please) that I shall never be capable of other resentment, than which shall witness the quality that I bear / Sir / of / your humble servant. (7)

This letter, here quoted in its entirety, was published in the 1640 translation of a book of model letters by Jean Puget de La Serre. Its form is contrived but not artful; its content, obsequious and shallow. It is not successful even as flattery, if clumsiness in the first sentence and redundancy in the second are any indication. Other blemishes: dull verbs (*give* thanks, *make* account, *render* respects); inadvertent ambiguity in the phrase *as making*, which looks at first as though it refers to the addressee, not the addressor; excessive embedding: the parenthetical phrases add little, like hiccups.

On the other hand, elevated social rank supplies incentives for aesthetic achievement or expertise. Lower-class prose may be graceful or not, but there is always some presumption that upper-class prose will aim at elegance and refinement. A consideration of some of the distinctive excellences of good courtly-genteel prose is therefore helpful in understanding the stylistics of social class in eighteenth-century prose, keeping in mind that each writer handles courtly-genteel conventions differently, and every text bears the stamp of its genre, date, context.

The aesthetic virtues of good courtly-genteel prose are not forcefulness, magnificence, or intensity, but gracefulness, complexity, tact, the ease that comes "from art not chance," irony. The syntax of good courtly prose is as much architectonic as linear; its goals are accomplished as often by artful indirection as by simple declaratives. It is at home with abstractions, deals frequently with abstract relationships, and reflects frequently upon itself. It values self-control above rapture, grace above power.[6]

Polite eighteenth-century letters are perhaps the most satisfying medium for courtly elegance in English prose, especially their closing sentences. According to inherited conventions, the writers of polite letters—and many of the so-called familiar letters of the seventeenth and eighteenth centuries were very polite—were obligated to declare themselves as *servant* of the person they were writing to in the valediction, immediately preceding the signature. The courtly relationship of extreme subservience between vassal and lord is revived however briefly or implausibly by the form of the valediction. That form greatly constrains the syntax of the last sentence or two of the letter: the name of the writer is the last word in the last sentence of the letter, and functions as a noun; how can it be most elegantly incorporated into the sweeping bow or curtsy with which addressors proclaim themselves the humble, faithful, or devoted servants of addressees?

The simplest way is a first-person statement with the verb *to be*:

> I am, Madam,
>   Your most obedient and humble servant,
>   [signature]

This can either be pared down to one or two words or expanded to take up half the letter. There is little room for variation in the pared-down version, "Yours sincerely" or "Your devoted servant" or a similar uninteresting formula. But formal excellence in courtly valedictions depends on elaboration, not simplification. It depends on the ingenuity and skill with which a writer expands the "I am your humble servant" formula and at the same time blends it with the preceding text so as to be functional, not added on. The letter must end with a declaration of devotion, but that declaration must grow organically out of the text that precedes it.

For example, the valediction may open with "I am" and then add qualifiers and variations to express affection or compliment the addressee:

> I am My Lord, with the sincerest respect
> Your most obliged & most
> faithfull Servant,
> A. Pope.
>
> (*Correspondence*, 2:307)

What has been added here is syntactically simple (a prepositional phrase, "with the sincerest respect," an extra adjective, "faithfull," and the two superlatives). This variation is capable of many further elaborations, as in the following by Pope:

I am
- with the Sincerest Esteem and most pleasing Obligation (2:336)
- and ever shall be (2:423)
- with faithful Esteem, with obligation, & Gratefulness (2:431)
- vastly more in Heart and Spirit, than in Powr or Act (2:527)
- (while I live) / My Lord (2:516)
- with the hope of sometimes hearing of your good health, ever My Lord (2:506)

In all these cases Pope has added something to the plain goodbye that ends a letter, something of his own affection or gratitude.

But not much skill is required to insert a few qualifiers between "I am" and the signature; for more elaborate valedictions, in which most of the sentence precedes the verb *to be* and complements the declaration of service—for something more fully formed and artful by indirection, we turn to letters by the fourth Earl of Chesterfield.

Chesterfield was a courtier in the old style: diplomat, man of letters, patron, and lord of the manor. A favorite courtly-genteel valediction in his letters is the "abstraction-with-which-I-am" formula. On this framework Chesterfield built graceful structures, the more pleasing when they do not insist too much but evolve unaffectedly out of concerns and topics other than the necessity of saying farewell.

For example, an early letter to the Honourable Mrs. Howard is both an exercise in high friendship and a courtier's bow of subservience to the mistress of George II. It opens with a compliment:

> Among the many privileges I enjoy here, I exercise none with so much pleasure as I do that which you granted me of writing to you, in order to put you sometimes in mind of a very humble servant, too insignificant to be remembered by anything but his importunity. (2:36)

Paragraphs two and three of this four-paragraph letter lightheartedly chronicle the amusements of The Hague, where Chesterfield had arrived eleven days previously for a four-year term of serious business as British ambassador. "After all this," he concludes,

> to speak seriously, I am very far from disliking this place: I have business enough one part of the day to make me relish the amusements of the other part, and even to make them seem pleasures; and if anything can comfort one for the absence of those one loves or esteems, it is meeting with the good will of those one is obliged to be with, which very fortunately, though undeservedly, is my case. There is, besides, one pleasure that I may have here, and that I own I am sanguine enough to expect, which will make me amends for the want of many others, which is, if you will have the goodness to let me know sometimes that you are well, and that you have not quite forgot that perfect esteem and respect with which I am,
> Yours, etc.
>
> (2:38)

In this valediction the harmony of parts and whole is almost complete: Chesterfield's *present* "esteem and respect" are offered in closing as tokens of *future* and continued friendship, and will therefore reappear in letters that he counts on as "amends for the want of" many such nonepistolary "pleasures" as have been the main topic of the letter he is writing now. The last paragraph echoes the first and capitalizes on the playful-but-serious narrative of the second and third. In a letter of powerful illocutionary dimensions—more an act of friendship than a description, a proposition, or an argument—the courtly valediction functions as a recapitulative cadence, a satisfying close.

I am not entirely happy with the syntax of Chesterfield's concluding sentence. Its grammatical subject, "one pleasure," is overburdened with relative clauses: "one pleasure that I may . . . and that I own . . . which will . . . which is." Then in later clauses *that* occurs both in indirect discourse and in an unexpected role as demonstrative adjective: "let me know that you are . . . and that you have . . . that esteem with which I am . . ." These are not distressing faults, but they suggest that the very finest courtly prose will be found in texts by people whose primary talent is writing, not diplomacy.

Samuel Johnson's letters supply examples of the finest courtly prose. Johnson prided himself on being a polite man, and his control of syntax—his ability to write complex sentences answering to complex abstract relationships—was unequaled (Wimsatt, 1941, 1948). He succeeds quite frequently in a feat of valediction that Pope and Chesterfield almost never attempt: shedding the obtrusive *I am* of the standard formula and incorporating the subscription, the noun phrase "your humble servant / Sam. Johnson," into a sentence that performs some other function than valediction. Genuine elegance, perhaps, is not a superficial attribute but derives from personal decorum, psychosocial health. In that case, outward expressions of genuine elegance will bear the stamp of inner loyalties. *Le style c'est l'homme même.* And so the sweeping bows stipulated by convention in polite letters of the eighteenth century must be at once natural and new; they must do the job brilliantly without calling attention to themselves.

Many of Johnson's best letters are, like Chesterfield's to Mrs. Howard, letters of friendship, the purpose of which is less to convey information or argue a case than simply to indicate affection. Unlike Chesterfield's letters, they list Johnson's achievements or satisfactions less often than they do his illnesses and self-doubts; but friendship itself is the most recurrent theme: indeed, the artfulness of Johnson's valedictions consists quite often of the manner in which he tucks his own name as subscriber into a sentence in praise of friendship:

you must be a patient creditor [if you expect answers to your letters]. I have however this of gratitude that I think of you with regard when I do not perhaps give the proofs which I ought of being,
>Sir, your most obliged and most
>humble servant

(1:40)

In the process of completing a letter which is itself an act of friendship, Johnson subscribes himself as less active in friendship than he wishes to be or than he urges his friend to be. Similarly, in his second letter to Boswell, which opens with yet another apology for being "such a sparing and ungrateful correspondent," Johnson opines that "The longer we live, and the more we think, the higher value we learn to put on the friendship and tenderness of parents and of friends."

> Parents we can have but once; and he promises himself too much, who enters life with the expectation of finding many friends. Upon some [such] motive, I hope that you will be here soon; and am willing to think that it will be an inducement to your return, that it is sincerely desired by, dear Sir, Your affectionate humble servant,
>> Sam: Johnson

(1:183–84)

Since these are letters of high friendship, there is a natural, logical relation between the topics they treat—the value of friendship, the desirability of reunions of friends—and the person writing; Johnson makes that connection and takes his leave, both operations at the same time, in a prepositional phrase. The effect is of courtly self-effacement, like a bow or curtsy undertaken as an integral part of the life of a courteous person.

The fact that courtly valedictions necessarily occur at the end of letters enables them to attempt a species of excellence more literally formal than others we have looked at. Out of the corner of their eyes, readers can sense the end of the letter approaching as they make their way down the page; they know that the writer will sign off as an "obedient servant"; they do not know what form that declaration will take; the nearer they get to the end without meeting that declaration or a signal announcing it—'I am . . .', or 'Permit me to assure you, madam', or 'I despair to tell you with how much sincerity, sir'—the more they wonder whether and how the writer will bring it off. Some sonnets get a more intense but comparable effect by playing the sense of the concluding couplet off against expectations aroused in the first twelve lines.

To illustrate this effect, here is a letter from Samuel Johnson to Elizabeth Montagu in its entirety:

> Madam, / Goodness so conspicuous as yours will be often solicited and perhaps sometimes solicited by those who have little pretension to your favour. It is now my turn to introduce a petitioner, but such as I have reason to believe you will think worthy of your notice. Mrs. Ogle who kept the musick-room in Soho Square, a woman who struggles with great industry for the support of eight children, hopes by a Benefit Concert to set herself free from a few debts, which she cannot otherwise discharge. She has, I know not why, so high an opinion of me as to believe that you will pay less regard to her application than to mine. You know, Madam, I am sure you know, how hard it is to deny, and therefore would not wonder at my compliance, though I were to suppress a motive which you know not, the vanity of being supposed to be of any importance to Mrs. Montagu. But though I may be willing to see the world deceived for my advantage, I am not deceived myself, for I know that Mrs. Ogle will owe whatever favours she shall receive from the patronage which we humbly entreat on this occasion, much more to your compassion for honesty in distress, than to the request of, Madam
> Your most obedient and most humble servant
> Sam: Johnson
>
> (1:125)

Modesty seems to play a crucial role in this letter. It is implied, inversely, by the compliments in the first, fifth, and sixth sentences, and it is openly expressed in the self-deprecations of the writer as one who has "little pretension to your favour" and cannot imagine why *his* intervention has been enlisted. I do not believe that Johnson felt, even in passing, as flattered by the prospects of influencing

Mrs. Montagu as he says here; this modesty is a courtly pose, an acting-out of the humility of the "humble servant." A pose, but not a piece of hypocrisy, since anyone who asks a favor puts him- or herself in a posture of supplication. What distinguishes this letter from hundreds of others are the tactics by which Johnson exhibits himself as suppliant and as patron at the same time: the last thing a suppliant wishes to make any noise about is his own worth, but it happens in this case that Johnson is a suppliant only because he has been successfully supplicated. His having granted a favor to Mrs. Ogle makes a comparison between him and the potential favor-granter he is writing to inevitable. Johnson uses the leverage he has extracted from that comparison ruthlessly but tactfully ("You know, Madam, *I am sure you know*, how hard it is to deny") to make Mrs. Montagu his accomplice in charity—and then backs away in the last sentence, protesting his own nothingness in comparison with her; that comparison provides the syntax by which he conjures himself into place at the end of the sentence: "*more* to your compassion . . . *than* the request of . . . Sam: Johnson."

To do justice to the elegance of the best courtly letters of the eighteenth century would require many more quotations, especially from Horace Walpole, whose essential gaiety and gallantry give him advantages over Johnson. For example, Walpole's letters to the Countess of Upper Ossory are brilliantly variegated, playful, witty, respectful, and affectionate; but never for an instant do they relax in courtesy, even at their silliest, or when written in sickness and pain. They demonstrate how much more there is to true gentility than bows and curtsies alone.

This context, affection and respect, explains why Johnson's most famous letter, the snub to Lord Chesterfield, is so unsettling. It begins with what might seem to be a conventional courtly protest of inadequacy. Chesterfield's recommendations are "an honour, which, being very little accustomed to favours from the Great, I know not well how to receive." Paragraphs two and three chronicle the lexicographer's unsuccessful addresses and his seven years of drudgery, "without one Act of assistance, one word of encouragement, or one smile of favour." Not satisfied with complaint alone, Johnson takes to the attack in paragraph five and lays about him vigorously, dispatching in quick succession the institution of patronage in general, Chesterfield's unhelpfulness in particular, and any notion whatsoever that Chesterfield's laudatory essays had put

Johnson in his debt. "I hope it is no very cynical asperity not to confess obligations where no benefit has been received" (1:64–65).

How to conclude such a letter? How can Johnson sign himself even *pro forma* as "obedient servant," after a declaration of independence so haughty and disobedient? By locating that conventional role and relation in the past:

> Having carried on my work thus far with so little obligation to any Favourer of Learning I shall not be disappointed though I should conclude it, if less be possible, with less, for I have been long wakened from that Dream of hope, in which I once boasted myself with so much exultation, My lord
>> Your Lordship's Most humble
>> Most Obedient Servant,
>> Sam: Johnson.

In the context of Chesterfield's charming letter to Mrs. Howard, Johnson's affectionate letters to Boswell, and the sincere respect Johnson shows both to Mrs. Ogle and to Mrs. Montague, this letter is almost shockingly angry and proud. Nevertheless, it is polite. It is not a lampoon. It maintains the *hauteur* of a courtier to the last; even as he asks whether it is humanly possible to owe less obligation than he does to Chesterfield, he confesses that the patronage that he was denied was a "Dream of hope" of which he once "boasted . . . with exultation." There's a compliment, if you will, but so completely negated by the renunciation of all dependency, that we may still stand amazed at Johnson's audacity. The elegance with which he performs the "compulsory figures" of a courtly letter enables him to confront the Earl as an equal, not simply as someone paying off an old grudge.

NOTES

1. Passages quoted in this paragraph are from J. C. Beaglehole's masterful "General Introduction" to James Cook's *The Voyage of the Endeavour*. The fact that Cook based some of his descriptions of Tahitian life on the manuscript journal of Joseph Banks, the gentleman-naturalist who accompanied him on this voyage, makes no difference to my analysis.

2. "My God! what shall I do?" "Why [discourse signal] what would

[archaic auxiliary] you do?" "Ma foi, Monsieur, I have lost my company, and in this place I don't know nobody" [double negative]. Mrs. Mirvan proposed to the Captain to assist her. "Assist her! [colloquial repetition, to accept a topic] Ay, with all my heart [colloquial asseveration];—let a link-boy call her a coach." Mrs. Mirvan reminded the Captain that the lady is a foreigner. "She's never the better for that [colloquial retort]; she may be a woman of the town, for anything you know [colloquial asseveration]. . . . You are mighty fond [archaic intensifier] of new acquaintance, but first let us know if she be going [archaic subjunctive] our way. . . . And pray, why did you go to a public place without an Englishman?" "Ma foi, Sir, because none of my acquaintance is in town." "Why then, I'll tell you what [retort discourteous], your best way is to go out of it yourself." "Pardie, Monsieur, and so I shall; for I promise you, I think the English a parcel of brutes; and I'll go back to France as fast as I can, for [overconcatenation] I would [archaic auxiliary] not live among none [double negative] of you." "Who wants you? do you suppose, Madame French, we have not enough of other nations to pick our pockets already? I'll warrant you, there's no need for you to put in your oar" [colloquial catch phrases and asseveration]. "Pick your pockets, Sir! [repetition for retort] I wish nobody wanted to pick your pockets no more [double negative] than I do; and I'll promise you, you'd be safe enough [colloquial asseveration]. But there's no nation under the sun can beat the English for ill-politeness [relative pronoun omitted]: for my part [topicalization], I hate the very sight of them, and so I shall only just visit a person of quality or two, of my particular acquaintance, and then I shall go back again to France." "Ay, do, and then go to the devil together [colloquial retort], for that's the fittest voyage for the French and the quality" (from Letter 14, 49–51).

3. Except that Sophia says *sure* for 'surely'. Selected examples of lower-class language in genteel characters in *Tom Jones*: "There is one only Way" (2:820; bk. 15, ch. 9); "whispered him . . . in the Ear" (2:713; bk. 13, ch. 7); "he writ . . . George . . . run" (2:980; bk. 18, ch. 13); "exceeding convenient" (2:827; bk. 15, ch. 11); "against it worked" (1:41; bk. 1, ch. 3). Fielding (like Richardson, though less obtrusively) uses the Elizabethan negative ("Mrs. *Fitzpatrick* failed not to make a proper Return") quite often, and his word order is more flexible, more seventeenth-century, than that of present-day speakers: "Thus run she on for near half an Hour" (2:891; bk. 17, ch. 4).

4. For a libertine courtly style in Lovelace, see William J. Farrell, "The Style and the Action in *Clarissa*," 365–75. For lively perspectives on style and social class in Richardson, Fielding, Defoe, and others, see Claude J. Rawson, "Language, Dialogue, and Point of View in Fielding: Some Considerations," 137–56. For Richardson's use of intonation and incremental repetition, see Irwin Gopnik, *A Theory of Style and Richardson's Clarissa*, 78–94. See also John Carroll, "Richardson at Work: Revisions, Allusions, and Quotations in *Clarissa*," especially pages 58–59.

Applications

5. Other examples: "exceeding great" (3:343, Mrs. Norton); "But yet I cannot tell you neither" (3:205, Clarissa); "enow" (3:25); "without" as a subordinate conjunction (3:388); and more double negatives (3:24, 183), all in Lovelace.

6. See Carey McIntosh, "Quantities of Qualities" (1975). For dextrous exploitation of complex, abstract sentences in comedy, see Norman Page, *The Language of Jane Austen*, 162–66.

BIBLIOGRAPHY

PRIMARY SOURCES

The Academy of Complements. London: Humphrey Mosley, 1640. STC 19882.8. Microfilm.

Amadis of Gaul. Translated by A. Munday. London, 1592? STC 541. Microfilm.

Anton, Robert. *Moromachia.* 1613. Reprinted in *Short Fiction of the Seventeenth Century*, edited by C. C. Mish. Garden City, N.Y.: Doubleday, 1963.

Arbuthnot, John. *The History of John Bull.* 1712. Edited by Alan W. Bower and Robert A. Erickson. London: Oxford University Press, 1976.

Armstrong, John [Launcelot Temple]. *Sketches.* In *Harrison's British Classicks*, vol. 8. London: Harrison & Co., 1787.

Ash, John. *Grammatical Institutes.* 1763. Reprint. Leeds: Scolar, 1967.

Ashton, J. *Chap-Books of the Eighteenth Century.* London: Chatto & Windus, 1882.

Austen, Jane. *Pride and Prejudice.* 1813. Edited by Tony Tanner. Harmondsworth: Penguin, 1972.

Baker, Robert. *Reflections on the English Language.* 1770. Reprint. Menston: Scolar, 1968.

Balzac, Jean Louis Guez de. *Les Premières Lettres . . . 1618−27.* Edited by H. Bibas and K.-T. Butler. Paris: E. Droz, 1933.

The Letters and Papers of the Banks Family of Revesby Abbey 1704−1760. Edited by J. W. F. Hill. Hereford: Lincoln Record Society, 1952.

Blackamore, Arthur. *Luck at Last; or, The Happy Unfortunate.* 1723. In *Four Before Richardson*, edited by W. H. McBurney. Lincoln, Nebr.: University of Nebraska Press, 1963.

Book of Common Prayer. New York: Oxford University Press, 1952.

Boswell, James. *Boswell's London Journal, 1762−1763.* Edited by F. A. Pottle. New York: McGraw Hill, 1950.

Brightland, John, and Charles Gildon. *A Grammar of the English Tongue.* 1711. Reprint. Menston: Scolar, 1967.

Buchanan, James. *A Regular English Syntax.* London: J. Wron, 1767.

Bunyan, John. *Grace Abounding to the Chief of Sinners.* Edited by Roger Sharrock. Oxford: Clarendon Press, 1962.

Burke, Edmund. *Correspondence.* Edited by T. W. Copeland. Chicago: University of Chicago Press, 1958−.

Burn, John. *A Practical Grammar of the English Language.* Glasgow: Archibald McLean, Jr., 1766.

Burney, Frances. *Evelina, or, the History of a Young Lady's Entrance into the World.* 1778. Reprint. Edited by Edward A. Bloom. London: Oxford University Press, 1968.

Butler, Joseph. *The Analogy of Religion.* 1736. Edited by Ernest C. Mossner. New York: Frederick Ungar, 1961.

Campbell, George. *The Philosophy of Rhetoric.* 1776. Edited by Lloyd F. Bitzer. Carbondale, Ill.: Southern Illinois University Press, 1963.

Capellanus, Andreas. *De amore libri tres.* Edited by A. Pagès. Castelló de la Plana: Sociedad castellonense de cultura, 1930.

Carter, Elizabeth. *Letters from Mrs. Elizabeth Carter, to Mrs. Montagu.* Edited by M. Pennington. London: F. C. Rivington, 1817.

———. *Memoirs of the Life of Mrs. Elizabeth Carter.* Edited by Rev. Montagu Pennington. 1807. 4th ed. London: J. Cawthorn, 1825.

Castiglione, Baldassare. *The Book of the Courtier.* Translated by Thomas Hoby. 1561. Reprint. London: J. M. Dent, 1928.

Caxton, William. Prologue to *Caton.* In *Fifteenth Century Prose and Verse,* edited by A. W. Pollard. New York: E. P. Dutton, 1903.

Chesterfield, Philip Dormer Stanhope, fourth Earl of. *Letters.* 6 vols. Edited by Bonamy Dobrée. London: Eyre & Spottiswoode, 1932.

Cicero, Marcus Tullius. *Essays on Old Age and Friendship. [Laelius.]* Translated by William Melmoth, 1773–77. 8th edition. London: Lackington, Hughes, 1820.

The Civile Conversation of M. Steeven Guazzo. Translated by George Pettie. 1581. Reprint. London: Constable, 1925.

Cook, James. *The Voyage of the Endeavour 1768–1771.* Edited by J. C. Beaglehole. Cambridge: Cambridge University Press, 1955.

Corneille, Pierre. *Théatre complet.* Edited by G. Couton. Paris: Garnier, 1971.

Courthope, James. *The Minute Book of James Courthope.* Edited by Orlo Cyprian Williams. Camden Miscellany 20 (Camden 3d Series 83). London: Butler & Tanner, 1953.

Cupids Schoole: Wherein Youngmen and Maids may Learne divers sorts of new, witty, and Amorous Complements. London, 1632.

Defoe, Daniel. *An Essay upon Projects.* 1697. In *Daniel Defoe,* edited by James T. Boulton. New York: Schocken, 1965.

———. *The Fortunes and Misfortunes of the Famous Moll Flanders.* 1722. Edited by G. A. Starr. London: Oxford University Press, 1971.

———. *The History . . . of . . . Col. Jacque.* Edited by S. H. Monk. London: Oxford University Press, 1965.

Dekker, Thomas. *The Gull's Horn-Book.* 1609. In *Thomas Dekker,* edited by E. D. Pendry. Cambridge, Mass.: Harvard University Press, 1968.

de la Calprenède, Gautier de Costes. *Pharamond.* Translated by J. Phillips. London, 1677.

Bibliography

Deloney, Thomas. *Thomas of Reading.* 1632. In *Shorter Novels: Elizabethan,* edited by G. Saintsbury and P. Henderson. New York: E. P. Dutton, 1929.

Dilworth, Thomas. *A New Guide to the English Tongue.* 1740. Reprint. Leeds: Scolar, 1967.

Dryden, John. "Dedication" to *Troilus.* 1679. In *The Critical Opinions of John Dryden,* edited by John M. Aden. Nashville: Vanderbilt University Press, 1963.

———. *Essay of Dramatic Poesy.* 1668. In *The Works of John Dryden,* vol. 17, edited by Samuel H. Monk. Berkeley: University of California Press, 1971.

d'Urfé, Honoré. *Les Epistres morales et amoureuses.* 1619. Reprint. Geneva, 1973.

Dyche, Thomas. *A Guide to the English Tongue.* 1707. Reprint. Menston: Scolar, 1968.

The English Accidence. 1733. Reprint. Leeds: Scolar, 1967.

Entick, John. *Speculum Latinum.* 1728. Reprint. Menston: Scolar, 1967.

Fenning, Daniel. *A New Grammar of the English Language.* 1771. Reprint. Menston: Scolar, 1967.

Fielding, Henry. *The Author's Farce.* 1730. Edited by C. Woods. Lincoln, Nebr.: University of Nebraska Press, 1966.

———. *The Champion.* 1740. In *Works,* edited by Leslie Stephen, vol. 5. London: Smith, Elder & Co., 1882.

———. *The History of Tom Jones A Foundling.* 1749. Edited by Martin Battestin and Fredson Bowers. 2 vols. Oxford: Wesleyan University Press, 1975.

———. *Joseph Andrews.* 1742. Edited by M. C. Battestin. Boston: Houghton Mifflin, 1961.

Fisher, Ann. *A New Grammar.* 1750. Reprint. Menston: Scolar, 1968.

Ford, John. *'Tis Pity She's a Whore.* 1633. Edited by H. Ellis. New York: Hill & Wang, 1957.

Fronto, Marcus Cornelius. *Correspondence.* Edited by C. R. Haines. Cambridge, Mass.: Harvard University Press, 1955.

Fulwood, William. *The Enimie of Idlenesse.* 1568. STC 11476. University Microfilms, no. 13998.

Gascoigne, George. *The Glasse of Governement.* 1575. In *Works,* vol. 2, edited by J. W. Cunliffe. Cambridge: Cambridge University Press, 1910.

Gough, James. *A Practical Grammar of the English Tongue.* 1754. Reprint. Menston: Scolar, 1967.

Greenwood, James. *An Essay towards a Practical English Grammar.* 1711. Reprint. Menston: Scolar, 1968.

Grose, Francis. *A Classical Dictionary of the Vulgar Tongue.* 1785. Reprint. Menston: Scolar, 1968.

Hall, Bishop Joseph. *Works.* Edited by J. Pratt. London: C. Whittingham, 1808.

Harris, James. *Hermes.* 1751. Reprint. Menston: Scolar, 1968.

Hawkesworth, John. *An Account of the Voyages . . . for Making Discoveries in the Southern Hemisphere.* 3 vols. London: W. Strahan & T. Cadell, 1773.

Head, Richard. *The English Rogue.* 1665. Edited by Michael Shinagel. Boston: New Frontiers, 1961.

Heywood, Eliza. *Philidore and Placentia.* 1727. In *Four Before Richardson,* edited by W. H. McBurney. Lincoln, Nebr.: University of Nebraska Press, 1963.

Howard, John. *The State of the Prisons in England and Wales.* Warrington: William Eyres, 1777.

The Jamaican Lady. 1720. Reprinted in *Four Before Richardson,* edited by W. H. McBurney. Lincoln, Nebr.: University of Nebraska Press, 1963.

Jewell, Joseph. *Autobiographical Memoir.* Edited by Arthur Walter Slater. Camden Miscellany 22 (Camden 4th Series 1). London: Butler & Tanner, 1964.

Johnson, Samuel. *A Dictionary of the English Language.* 2 vols. 1755. Reprint. New York: AMS Press, 1967. Includes "Preface," "History of the Language," "Grammar."

―――. *Johnson on Shakespeare.* Edited by Arthur Sherbo. 2 vols. New Haven: Yale University Press, 1968. Includes *Proposals* (1756), *Preface* and *Notes* (1765).

―――. *A Journey to the Western Islands of Scotland.* Edited by Mary Lascelles. New Haven: Yale University Press, 1971.

―――. *Letters.* Edited by R. W. Chapman. 3 vols. Oxford: Clarendon Press, 1952.

―――. *The Plan of a Dictionary of the English Language.* 1747. Reprint. Menston: Scolar, 1970.

―――. *The Works of Samuel Johnson, Ll.D.* 9 [11] vols. Oxford: Wm. Pickering, 1825.

Jones, Hugh. *An Accidence to the English Tongue.* 1724. Reprint. Menston: Scolar, 1967.

Jonson, Ben. *Timber; or Discoveries.* 1641. Edited by Israel Gollancz. London: J. M. Dent, 1951.

The Letters of Junius. 1769. Edited by John Cannon. Oxford: Clarendon Press, 1978.

Kames, Henry Home, Lord. *Elements of Criticism.* 1762. Reprint. New York: Huntington & Savage, 1842.

Killigrew, Thomas. *Comedies and Tragedies.* 1664. Reprint. New York: B. Blom, 1967.

Kirkby, John. *A New English Grammar.* 1746. Reprint. Menston: Scolar, 1971.

Lane, A. *A Key to the Art of Letters.* 1700. Reprint. Menston: Scolar, 1969.

La Serre, Jean Puget de. *The Secretary in Fashion.* Translated by J. Massinger. 1640. Rev. ed. London: H. Moseley, 1654.

Bibliography

Law, William. *A Serious Call to a Devout and Holy Life.* 1728. Edited by Norman Sykes. London: J. M. Dent, 1906.

Liturgies and Occasional Forms of Prayer Set Forth in the Reign of Queen Elizabeth. Edited by W. K. Clay. Cambridge: Cambridge University Press, 1847.

Locke, John. *An Essay concerning Human Understanding.* 1690. Edited by Alexander C. Fraser. 2 vols. 1894. Reprint. New York: Dover, 1959.

Loughton, William. *A Practical Grammar of the English Tongue.* London: C. Ward, 1734.

Lowth, Robert. *A Short Introduction to English Grammar.* 1762. Reprint. Menston: Scolar, 1967.

McBurney, William H. *Four Before Richardson: Selected English Novels, 1720–1727.* Lincoln: University of Nebraska Press, 1963.

Malory, Thomas. *Works.* Edited by Eugene Vinaver. London: Oxford University Press, 1954.

Mandeville, Bernard. *The Fable of the Bees.* 1714. Edited by Irwin Primer. New York: Capricorn Books, 1962.

Manley, Delarivière. *The Secret History of Queen Zarah.* 1705. 2 vols. Reprint. Gainesville, Fla.: Scholar's Facsimiles, 1971.

Melmoth, William, trans. *The Letters of Pliny the Consul.* 8th ed. London: J. Dodsley, 1786.

Montaigne, Michel de. *Oeuvres complètes.* Edited by A. Thibaudet and M. Rat. Paris: Gallimard, 1962.

More, Thomas. *Selected Letters.* Edited by E. F. Rogers. New Haven: Yale University Press, 1961.

Morindos, The History of. 1609. In *Short Fiction of the Seventeenth Century*, edited by C. C. Mish. Garden City, N.Y.: Doubleday, 1963.

Murray, Lindley. *English Grammar.* 1795. Reprint. Menston: Scolar, 1968.

Nashe, Thomas. *Pierce Penilesse his Supplication to the Devil.* 1592. In *Thomas Nashe . . . Selected Writings*, edited by Stanley Wells. London: Edward Arnold, 1964.

———. *The Unfortunate Traveler.* In *Elizabethan Fiction*, edited by R. Ashley and E. M. Mosely. New York: Holt, Rinehart & Winston, 1953.

Nelson, John. *The Case of John Nelson.* 1745. Reprint. New York: Garland, 1974.

Original Letters, Illustrative of English History. Edited by Henry Ellis. 3 vols. 1st ser. London: Harding, 1825.

Osborne, Dorothy. *The Letters of Dorothy Osborne to William Temple.* Edited by G. C. Moore Smith. Oxford: Clarendon Press, 1928.

Paine, Thomas. *The Rights of Man.* 1791. Edited by Israel Gollancz. London: J. M. Dent, 1951.

Paston Letters. Edited by J. Warrington. 2 vols. London: J. M. Dent, 1956.

Penn, William. *Some Fruits of Solitude.* 1693. Rev. ed. 1718. Edited by Edmund Gosse. New York: Truslove, Hanson, & Comba, 1900.

Petrie, Adam. *Rules of Good Deportment, or of Good Breeding.* 1720. Reprint. Edinburgh, 1835.

Pettie, George. *A Petite Pallace of Pettie his Pleasure.* 1576. Edited by H. Hartman. London: Oxford University Press, 1938.

Phillips, Edward. *The Mysterie of Love and Eloquence, or, the Arts of Wooing and Complementing.* London: N. Brooks, 1658.

Plimpton, George A. *Out of My League.* 1961. Reprint. New York: Pocket Books, 1967.

Pope, Alexander. *Correspondence.* Edited by George Sherburn. 5 vols. Oxford: Clarendon Press, 1956.

Priestley, Joseph. *The Rudiments of Grammar.* 1761. Reprint. Menston: Scolar, 1969.

Pulteney, William [Caleb D'Anvers, pseud.]. *The Craftsman.* "By Caleb D'Anvers." 1726. Reprint. London: R. Francklin, 1731.

Reeve, Clara. *The Progress of Romance.* 1785. Reprint. New York: The Facsimile Text Society, 1930.

Richardson, Samuel. *Clarissa; or, The History of a Young Lady.* 1748. Reprint in 4 vols. London: J. M. Dent, 1962.

———. *Familiar Letters on Important Occasions.* 1741. Edited by Brian W. Downs. London: G. Routledge, 1928.

———. *The History of Sir Charles Grandison.* Oxford: Basil Blackwell, 1931.

———. *Pamela.* 1740. Edited by W. M. Sale. New York: Norton, 1958.

Rogers, Francis. *Diary.* 1701–1704. In *Three Sea Journals of Stuart Times*, edited by Bruce S. Ingram. London: Constable, 1936.

Rousseau, Jean-Jacques. *Confessions.* Translated by J. M. Cohen. Harmondsworth: Penguin, 1954.

Saxon, Samuel. *The English Scholar's Assistant.* 1737. Reprint. Menston: Scolar, 1971.

Segar, Sir William. *Honor Military and Civill.* London: R. Barker, 1602. STC 22164. Microfilm.

Seven Champions of Christendom. London: C. Burbie, 1596. STC 14677. Microfilm.

Shaftesbury, Anthony Ashley Cooper, third Earl of. *Characteristics of Men, Manners, Opinions, Times.* 1711. Edited by John M. Robertson. Indianapolis: Bobbs-Merrill, 1964.

Shakespeare, William. *The Riverside Shakespeare.* Edited by G. Blakemore Evans. Boston: Houghton Mifflin, 1974.

Shardeloes Papers of the 17th and 18th Centuries. Edited by G. Eland. London: Oxford University Press, 1947.

Sheridan, Richard Brinsley. *The Rivals.* 1775. In *Eighteenth-Century Plays*, edited by Ricardo Quintana. New York: Random House, 1952.

Shirley, James. *Love Tricks.* 1625. In *The Dramatic Works and Poems*, edited by W. Gifford and A. Dyce, 6 vols. London: J. Murray, 1833.

Sidney, Sir Philip. *Complete Works.* Edited by A. Feuillerat. 3 vols. Cambridge: Cambridge University Press, 1923.

Bibliography

————. *The Countesse of Pembrokes Arcadia*. 1596. Edited by A. Feuillerat. Cambridge: Cambridge University Press, 1912.

Smollett, Tobias. *The Expedition of Humphry Clinker*. 1771. Edited by Lewis M. Knapp. London: Oxford University Press, 1966.

Spence, Joseph. *Letters from the Grand Tour*. Edited by Slava Klima. Montreal: McGill-Queen's University Press, 1975.

Swift, Jonathan. *A Complete Collection of Genteel and Ingenious Conversation, According to the Most Polite Mode and Method Now used At Court*. 1738. Edited by G. Saintsbury. London: Whittingham, 1892.

————. *A Proposal for Correcting, Improving and Ascertaining the English Tongue*. 1712. Reprint. Menston: Scolar, 1969.

————. *A Tale of a Tub*. 1710. In *Gulliver's Travels and Other Writings*, edited by Louis A. Landa. Boston: Houghton Mifflin, 1960.

————. *The Tatler, No. 230*. 1710. In *Gulliver's Travels and Other Writings*, edited by Louis A. Landa. Boston: Houghton Mifflin, 1960.

Temple, Sir William. *Works*. 1814. Reprint. New York: Greenwood Press, 1968.

Thrale, Hester Lynch. *The Family Book*. 1764–78. In Mary Hyde, *The Thrales of Streatham Park*. Cambridge, Mass.: Harvard University Press, 1977.

Vaugelas, Claude Favre de. *Remarques sur la langue francoise*. 1647. Reprint. Paris: Droz, 1934, 1970.

Verney Letters of the Eighteenth Century: from the MSS at Claydon House. Edited by Margaret Maria Lady Verney. London: Ernest Benn, 1930.

Voiture, Vincent. *Familiar and Courtly Letters to Persons of the Greatest Honour*. London: S. Briscoe, 1700.

Voltaire. *Correspondence*. In *Les oeuvres complètes de Voltaire*, edited by Theodore Besterman, vol. 101. Banbury: Voltaire Foundation, 1971.

Walpole, Horace. *Correspondence*. Edited by W. S. Lewis. Vol. 32, *The Countess of Upper Ossory*. New Haven: Yale University Press, 1965.

Ward, Ned. *The London Spy*. 1698. Edited by Ralph Straus. London: Casanova Soc., 1924.

Wesley, John. *An Earnest Appeal to Men of Reason and Religion*. 1743. In *Works*, edited by Gerald R. Cragg, vol. 2. Oxford: Clarendon Press, 1975.

————. *Short English Grammar*. Bristol, 1748.

Whitefield, George. *A Short Account of God's Dealings with the Reverend Mr. George Whitefield, A.B.* 1740. Edited by William M. Davis. Gainesville, Fla.: Scholars Facsimiles & Reprints, 1969.

Secondary Sources

Abbott, Edwin Abbott. *A Shakespearian Grammar*. London: Macmillan, 1872.

Adams, George Burton. "Feudalism." *Encyclopaedia Britannica.* 14th ed. London, 1929.

Adolph, Robert. *The Rise of Modern Prose Style.* Cambridge, Mass.: MIT Press, 1968.

Allen, Harold B. "Samuel Johnson and the Authoritarian Principle in Linguistic Criticism." Ph.D. diss., University of Michigan, 1940 (as cited by Sledd, 37).

Alston, R. C. *A Bibliography of the English Language.* Vol. 1, *English Grammars Written in England.* Leeds: E. J. Arnold & Son, 1965.

Auerbach, Erich. *Mimesis: The Representation of Reality in Western Literature.* Translated by Willard Trask. 1946. Garden City, N.Y.: Anchor, 1957.

Baker, Ernest A. *A History of the English Novel.* London: Witherby, 1929.

Baker, Sheridan. "Evil, Primitivism, and Progress in Gibbon's *Decline and Fall.*" *Modern Language Studies* 10 (1980):32–42.

———. "*Humphry Clinker* as Comic Romance." *Papers of the Michigan Academy of Science, Arts and Letters* 46 (1961):645–54.

———. "The Idea of Romance in the Eighteenth-Century Novel." *Papers of the Michigan Academy of Science, Arts and Letters* 49 (1964):507–22.

Barish, Jonas A. *Ben Jonson and the Language of Prose Comedy.* Cambridge, Mass.: Harvard University Press, 1960.

Baron, Naomi. *Speech, Writing, and Sign.* Bloomington: Indiana University Press, 1981.

Bate, Walter Jackson. *The Achievement of Samuel Johnson.* New York: Oxford University Press, 1955.

Baugh, Albert C. *A History of the English Language.* 2d. ed. New York: Appleton-Century-Crofts, 1957.

Beasley, Jerry C. *Novels of the 1740s.* Athens, Ga.: University of Georgia Press, 1982.

Bernstein, Basil. *Class, Codes and Control.* London: Routledge & Kegan Paul, 1971.

Bickerton, Derek. *Dynamics of a Creole System.* Cambridge: Cambridge University Press, 1975.

Bloch, Marc. *Feudal Society.* Translated by L. A. Manyon. 1961. Chicago: University of Chicago Press.

Boggs, W. Arthur. "A Win Jenkins Lexikon." *Bulletin of the New York Public Library* 68 (1964):323–30.

Boulton, James T. "Daniel Defoe: His Language and Rhetoric." In *Daniel Defoe,* edited by James T. Boulton. New York: Schocken, 1965.

Brewer, D. S. "Courtesy and the *Gawain*-Poet." In *Patterns of Love and Courtesy,* edited by John Lawlor. Evanston: Northwestern University Press, 1966.

Brook, Stella. *The Language of the Book of Common Prayer.* New York: Oxford University Press, 1965.

Brown, Roger, and Albert Gilman. "The Pronouns of Power and Solidarity." In *Style in Language*, edited by Thomas A. Sebeok. Cambridge, Mass.: MIT Press, 1960.

Carroll, John. "Richardson at Work: Revisions, Allusions, and Quotations in *Clarissa*." In *Studies in the Eighteenth Century*, edited by R. F. Brissenden. Toronto: University of Toronto Press, 1973.

Cecil, C. D. "'Une Espèce d'Eloquence Abrégée,' The Idealized Speech of Restoration Comedy." *Etudes Anglaises* 19 (1966):15–25.

Chafe, Wallace L. "Givenness, Contrastiveness, Definiteness, Subjects, Topics, and Point of View." In *Subject and Topic*, edited by Charles Li. New York: Academic Press, 1976.

Chandler, Frank W. *The Literature of Roguery*. 2 vols. Boston: Houghton, Mifflin, 1907.

Clifford, James L. *Dictionary Johnson: Samuel Johnson's Middle Years*. New York: McGraw-Hill, 1979.

Cohen, Murray. *Sensible Words: Linguistic Practice in England 1640–1785*. Baltimore: Johns Hopkins University Press, 1977.

Cowler, Rosemary. "Shadow and Substance: A Discussion of Pope's Correspondence." In *The Familiar Letter in the Eighteenth Century*, edited by P. B. Daghlian. Lawrence, Kans.: University of Kansas Press, 1966.

Cressy, David. *Literacy and the Social Order: Reading and Writing in Tudor and Stuart England*. Cambridge: Cambridge University Press, 1980.

Croll, Morris W. *Style, Rhetoric, and Rhythm*. Edited by J. Max Patrick. Princeton, N.J.: Princeton University Press, 1966.

Crystal, David, and Derek Davy. *Investigating English Style*. Bloomington: Indiana University Press, 1969.

Daghlian, Philip B. "Dr. Johnson in his Letters: the Public Guise of Private Matter." In *The Familiar Letter in the Eighteenth Century*, edited by H. Anderson, P. B. Daghlian, and I. Ehrenpreis. Lawrence, Kans.: University of Kansas Press, 1966.

Davis, Norman. "Style and Stereotype in Early English Letters." *Leeds Studies in English* n.s. 1 (1967):7–17.

Denomy, Alexander J. "Courtly Love and Courtliness." *Speculum* 28 (1953):44–63.

Dixon, R. M. W. *The Dyirbal Language of North Queensland* [Australia]. Cambridge: Cambridge University Press, 1972.

Duggan, G. C., *The Stage Irishman*. London: Longmans, Green, 1937.

Ehrenpreis, Irvin. "The Styles of *Gulliver's Travels*." In *Literary Learning and Augustan Values*. Charlottesville, Va.: University of Virginia Press, 1974.

———. *Swift: The Man, His Works, and the Age*. Vol. 1, *Dr. Swift*. London: Methuen, 1967.

Emerson, Oliver F. "John Dryden and a British Academy." *Proceedings of the British Academy* 10 (1921):45–58.

Farrell, William J. "The Style and the Action in *Clarissa*." *Studies in English Literature* 3 (1963):365–75.

Flanders, W. Austin. *Structures of Experience: History, Society, and Personal Life in the Eighteenth-Century British Novel.* Columbia: University of South Carolina Press, 1984.

Fowler, John. "Dryden and Literary Good-breeding." In *Restoration Literature: Critical Approaches,* edited by Harold Love. London: Methuen, 1972.

Franz, Wilhelm. *Shakespeare-Grammatik.* Halle: Max Niemeyer, 1900.

Gardiner, Frank C. *The Pilgrimage of Desire.* Leiden: Brill, 1971.

Gopnik, Irwin. *A Theory of Style and Richardson's Clarissa.* The Hague: Mouton, 1970.

Grimes, Joseph. "Introduction." In *Papers on Discourse.* Dallas: Summer Institute of Linguistics Publication 51, 1978.

Gumperz, John Joseph. *Discourse Strategies.* Cambridge: Cambridge University Press, 1982.

Halliday, Michael A. K. *System and Function in Language.* London: Oxford University Press, 1976.

Hatlen, Burton. "The Quest for the Concrete Particular, or Do Poets Have Something to Say to Sociolinguists?" In *Rhetoric 78: Proceedings of Theory of Rhetoric, an Interdisciplinary Conference,* edited by Robert L. Brown, Jr., and Martin Steinmann, Jr. Minneapolis: University of Minnesota Center for Advanced Studies in Language, Style, and Literary Theory, 1979.

Hornbeak, Katherine Gee. *The Complete Letter-Writer in English, 1568–1800.* Northampton, Mass.: Smith College Press, 1934.

Howell, Wilbur Samuel. *Eighteenth-Century British Logic and Rhetoric.* Princeton, N.J.: Princeton University Press, 1971.

Hyde, Mary. *The Thrales of Streatham Park.* Cambridge, Mass.: Harvard University Press, 1977.

James, Eustace Anthony. *Daniel Defoe's Many Voices: A Rhetorical Study of Prose Style and Literary Method.* Amsterdam, 1972.

Jeffrey, David L. "The Friar's Rent." *Journal of English and German Philology* 70 (1971):600–606.

Jespersen, Otto. "Syntax." Part 3 of *A Modern English Grammar.* Vol. 2. Heidelberg: C. Winter, 1927.

Jewson, Jan, J. Sachs, and R. Rohner. "The Effect of a Narrative Context on the Verbal Style of Middle-Class and Lower-Class Children." *Language in Society* 10 (1981):201–15.

Kay, Paul. "Language Evolution and Speech Style." In *Sociocultural Dimensions of Language Change,* edited by Ben G. Blount. New York: Academic Press, 1977.

Keenan, Edward L. "Towards a Universal Definition of 'Subject.'" In *Subject and Topic,* edited by C. Li. New York: Academic Press, 1976.

Klein, Lawrence. "The Third Earl of Shaftesbury and the Progress of Politeness." *Eighteenth-Century Studies* 18 (1984–85):186–214.

Bibliography

Krings, Hans. *Die Geschichte des Wortschatzes der Höflichkeit im Französischen.* Bonn: Romanisches Seminar der Universität Bonn, 1961.

Labov, William. *Sociolinguistic Patterns.* Philadelphia: University of Pennsylvania Press, 1972.

Laslett, Peter. "The Wrong Way Through the Telescope: a Note on Literary Evidence in Sociology and Historical Sociology." *British Journal of Sociology* 27 (1976):319–42.

Leclerq, Jean. "L'Amitié dans les Lettres au Moyen Age." *Revue du Moyen Age Latin* 1 (1945):391–410.

Leech, Geoffrey N., and Michael H. Short. *Style in Fiction: A Linguistic Introduction to English Fictional Prose.* New York: Longman, 1981.

Leonard, Sterling Andrus. *The Doctrine of Correctness in English Usage 1700–1800.* University of Wisconsin Studies in Language and Literature, 25. Madison: University of Wisconsin Press, 1929.

Li, Charles, ed. *Subject and Topic.* New York: Academic Press, 1976.

Li, Charles, and Sandra Thompson. "Subject and Topic: A New Typology of Language." In *Subject and Topic*, edited by C. Li. New York: Academic Press, 1976.

Live, Anna H. "The *Take-Have* Phrasal in English." *Linguistics* 95 (1973): 31–50.

Lodge, David. *Language of Fiction.* New York: Columbia University Press, 1966.

Marchand, Hans. *The Categories and Types of Present-Day English Word-Formation.* Wiesbaden: O. Harrassowitz, 1960.

Marshall, Dorothy. *The English Domestic Servant in History.* Historical Association Publications G 13. London: G. Philip & Son, 1949.

Mason, John E. *Gentlefolk in the Making: Studies in the History of English Courtesy Literature . . . 1531 to 1774.* Philadelphia: University of Pennsylvania Press, 1935.

Matthews, William. "Polite Speech in the Eighteenth Century." *English* 1 (1937):493–511.

McIntosh, Carey. "Quantities of Qualities: Nominal Style in the Novel." In *Studies in Eighteenth-Century Culture*, vol. 4, edited by H. Pagliaro. Madison: University of Wisconsin Press, 1975.

———. "The Evolution of Subordinate Conjunctions in English." MS.

Michael, Ian. *English Grammatical Categories.* Cambridge: Cambridge University Press, 1970.

Milic, Louis T. "Against the Typology of Styles." In *Essays on the Language of Literature*, edited by Seymour Chatman and S. R. Levin. Boston: Houghton Mifflin, 1967.

Mingay, G. E. *English Landed Society in the Eighteenth Century.* London: Routledge & Kegan Paul, 1963.

———. *The Gentry.* London: Longman, 1976.

Monroe, B. S. "An English Academy." *Modern Philology* 8 (1911):107–22.

Nist, John. *A Structural History of English.* New York: St. Martin's Press, 1966.

Ohmann, Richard. "Generative Grammars and the Concept of Literary Style." *Word* 20 (1964):423–39.

Page, Norman. *The Language of Jane Austen.* Oxford: Basil Blackwell, 1972.

Partridge, A. C. *Tudor to Augustan English.* London: Deutsch, 1969.

Partridge, Eric. *A Dictionary of Slang and Unconventional English.* 7th ed. New York: Macmillan, 1970.

Phillipps, K. C. "Lucy Steele's English." *English Studies* 50 (1969):Supplement lv–lxi.

Platt, Joan. "The Development of English Colloquial Idiom during the Eighteenth Century." *Review of English Studies* 2 (1926):70–81, 189–96.

Potter, Simeon. "English Language." *The New Encyclopaedia Britannica.* 15th ed. Chicago: University of Chicago Press, 1975.

Price, Cecil. "'The Art of Pleasing': The Letters of Chesterfield." In *The Familiar Letter in the Eighteenth Century,* edited by P. B. Daghlian. Lawrence, Kans.: University of Kansas Press, 1966.

Quirk, Randolph, Sidney Greenbaum, Geoffrey Leech, and Jan Svartvik. *A Grammar of Contemporary English.* London: Longman, 1972.

Rawson, Claude J. "Language, Dialogue, and Point of View in Fielding: Some Considerations." In *Quick Springs of Sense,* edited by L. S. Champion. Athens, Ga.: University of Georgia Press, 1974.

Richetti, John J. *Popular Fiction before Richardson.* London: Oxford University Press, 1969.

Rockinger, Ludwig. *Briefsteller und formelbücher des eilften bis vierzehnten jahrhunderts.* 2 vols. 1863. Reprint. New York: B. Franklin, 1961.

Sacks, Harvey, E. A. Schegloff, and G. Jefferson. "A Simple Systematics for the Organization of Turn-Taking for Conversation." *Language* 50 (1974):696–735.

Sherburn, George. "The Restoration and Eighteenth Century." In *A Literary History of England,* edited by A. C. Baugh. New York: Appleton-Century-Crofts, 1948.

Shinagel, Michael. *Daniel Defoe and Middle-Class Gentility.* Cambridge, Mass.: Harvard University Press, 1968.

Sledd, James H., and Gwin J. Kolb. *Dr. Johnson's Dictionary.* Chicago: University of Chicago Press, 1955.

Spitzer, Leo. *Linguistics and Literary History.* Princeton, N.J.: Princeton University Press, 1948.

Strang, Barbara M. H. *A History of English.* London: Methuen, 1970.

———. "Swift and the English Language: A Study in Principles and Practice." In *To Honor Roman Jakobson. Essays on the Occasion of His Seventieth Birthday,* vol. 3. The Hague: Mouton, 1967.

Strauss, Albrecht. "On Smollett's Language: A Paragraph in *Ferdinand Count Fathom.*" In *Style in Prose Fiction,* edited by Harold C. Martin. New York: Columbia University Press, 1959.

Bibliography

Sutherland, James. *On English Prose*. Toronto: University of Toronto Press, 1957.

Thompson, Edward P. *The Making of the English Working Class*. 1963. Reprint. New York: Random House, 1966.

Traugott, Elizabeth Closs, and Mary Louise Pratt. *Linguistics for Students of Literature*. New York: Harcourt Brace Jovanovich, 1980.

Treiman, Donald J. *Occupational Prestige in Comparative Perspective*. New York: Academic Press, 1977.

Trudgill, Peter. *The Social Differentiation of English In Norwich*. Cambridge: Cambridge University Press, 1974.

Watt, Ian. *The Rise of the Novel*. Berkeley: University of California Press, 1957.

Wimsatt, William K. *Philosophic Words: A Study of Style and Meaning in the Rambler and Dictionary of Johnson*. New Haven: Yale University Press, 1948.

———. *The Prose Style of Samuel Johnson*. New Haven: Yale University Press, 1941.

Wyld, Henry Cecil. *A History of Modern Colloquial English*. New York: E. P. Dutton, 1920.

INDEX

Index

Clarendon, Edward Hyde, 1st Earl of, 53
Clay, W. K., 100n
Cohen, Murray, 66n
Coleridge, Samuel T., 74
Collier, Jeremy, 38
Collyer, John, 47
Conditionals, 32, 130
Cook, Captain James, 64, 105–14, 145n
Corbet, James, 47
Corneille, Pierre, 95, 101n
Courthope, James, 17
Cowler, Rosemary, 100n
Cranmer, Thomas, 92
Cressy, David, 8
Croll, Morris, 10
Crystal, David, 6
Cupids Schoole, 86

d'Urfé, Honoré, 95, 101n
Datives, 32, 51, 104, 111, 146n
Davies, John, 87
Davy, Derek, 6
De la Calprenède, Gautier de Costes, 90–91
Defoe, Daniel, 10, 13, 15, 22–36, 37, 39–42, 44, 63, 102, 119, 146n
Dekker, Thomas, 74
Deloney, Thomas, 80
Denomy, Alexander J., 100n
Dialect, 121–23, 132–33, 135
Dicey, Cluer, 3, 15
Dilworth, Thomas, 48, 49, 51, 67n
Discourse signals, 24
Dixon, R. M. W., 65n
Donne, John, 14
Dryden, John, 10, 12, 39, 41–45, 50, 53, 56, 63, 64, 66n, 87, 118
Du Cange's *Glossarium*, 94
Duggan, G. C., 122
Dyche, Thomas, 49, 66n

Ehrenpreis, Irvin, 10
Emerson, Oliver, 39
Entick, John, 51, 67n
Evelyn, John, 39

Farrell, William J., 146n
Fenning, Daniel, 46
Fielding, Henry, 51; *The Author's Farce*, 74; *Joseph Andrews*, 71, 80–81; *Tom Jones*, 8, 33, 39, 43, 81, 85, 91, 118–23, 146n
Fisher, Ann, 49, 50, 67n
Flanders, W. Austin, 40
Ford, John, 75
Fortunatus, 3
Fowler, John, 66n
Franz, Wilhelm, 65n
Fronto, Marcus Cornelius, 100n
Fulwood, William, 86

Gardiner, Frank C., 100n
Gascoigne, George, 75
Gildon, Charles, 49–50, 66n
Gilman, Albert, 130
Gopnik, Irwin, 146n
Gough, James, 51
Greenwood, James, 47, 50–51, 66n
Grimes, Joseph, 65n
Grose, Francis, 23
Gumperz, John Joseph, 65n, 122

Hall, Bishop Joseph, 92
Halliday, Michael A. K., 65n
Harris, James, 48, 53
Hatlen, Burton, 11n
Hawkesworth, John, 105–14
Head, Richard, 3, 65n
Heywood, Eliza, 100n
Hickes, George, 53
Hoby, Thomas, 85
Home, Henry, Lord Kames, 46–47, 50–52, 55, 56, 59, 60, 63–64
Hook, Robert, 56
Hooker, Richard, 61
Horace, 14
Hornbeak, Katherine, 87, 100n
Howard, John, 13
Hume, David, 56
Hyde, Mary, 104

Impersonals, 20, 51

Index

Intensifyers, 18, 34, 55, 103, 104, 111, 146 n
Irregular verbs, 48, 51, 58, 66 n, 108, 146 n

James, Eustace Anthony, 64 n
Jeffrey, David, 100 n
Jespersen, Otto, 32, 68 n
Jewell, Joseph, 21–22
Jewson, Jan, 11 n
Johnson, Samuel: *Dictionary*, 17, 45–47, 56–59, 65 n, 68 n, 102–3, 109–11; *Journey*, 73; *Plan of Dictionary*, 39; Preface to *Dictionary*, 38, 40, 56, 62; prose style, 33, 51–53, 141–45; *Rambler*, 85; on Shakespeare, 59
Jones, Hugh, 50, 67 n
Jonson, Ben, 10, 12
Junius, 13

Kay, Paul, 11 n
Keenan, Edward L., 65 n
Killigrew, Thomas, 89, 91
King James Bible, 38, 53, 54, 65 n, 66 n
Kirkby, John, 47, 51
Kolb, Gwin J., 56, 103
Krings, Hans, 10

L'Estrange, Roger, 38
Labov, William, 9
Lane, A., 46–49, 66 n
La Serre, Jean Puget de, 137
Laslett, Peter, 5
Law, William, 13
Leclerq, Jean, 94
Leech, Geoffrey, 10
Leonard, S. A., 59, 102–3
Letters, prose style of, 70, 71, 138–45
Li, Charles, 65 n
Live, Anna, 133
Locke, John, 64, 66 n, 104–5
Lodge, David, 10
Loughton, William, 51, 67 n
Lovel, Lord John, 75
Lowth, Robert, 16–20, 22, 46–60,

62–64, 68 n, 102, 103, 109, 129, 133
Luck at Last, 77

McBurney, William H., 80
McIntosh, Carey, 58, 65 n, 147 n
Malory, Thomas, 95–97
Mandeville, Bernard, 13
Manley, Delarivière, 81–82
Marana, Giovanni, 14
Marchand, Hans, 133
Mason, John E., 85
Matthews, William, 10 n
Melmoth, William, 83–84, 100 n
Michael, Ian, 38, 47
Middleton, Conyers, 53
Milton, John, 53, 61, 83
Mingay, G. E., 7
Monroe, B. S., 119
Montagu, Elizabeth, 143
Montaigne, Michel de, 95, 101 n
More, Thomas, 82
Morindos, The History of, 100 n
Mulcaster, Richard, 56
Murray, Lindley, 54, 102, 103

Nashe, Thomas, 14, 79–80
Negatives, 35, 49, 103, 130, 133, 146 n
Nelson, John, 20
Nist, John, 65 n
North American Review, 18

Ohmann, Richard, 10
Osborne, Dorothy, 100 n
Oxford English Dictionary (*OED*), 16, 17, 18, 33, 34, 36, 58, 66 n, 79, 94, 102

Page, Norman, 147 n
Paine, Thoms, 13
Partridge, A. C., 66 n
Partridge, Eric, 17, 20, 57
Paston, William, 71
Paston Letters, 76, 97
Penn, William, 13
Petrie, Adam, 86

Index

Index

Tillotson, John, 53, 54
Tooke, Horne, 102
Topicalization, 26−27, 113, 146n
Trudgill, Peter, 11n

Vanderbilt, Amy, 88
Vaugelas, Claude Favre de, 39
Verney Letters, 10n, 20, 99
Voiture, Vincent, 87
Voltaire, 40

Wallis, John, 66n
Walpole, Horace, 12, 144

Ward, John, 53
Ward, Ned, 14
Watt, Ian, 10, 64n
Webster, Noah, 102, 103
Wesley, John, 13, 47
Whitefield, George, 13
Wilkins, John, 53
Wimsatt, William K., 10, 141
Word order, 21, 49, 51, 111, 130, 133, 146n
Wycherley, Sir William, 83
Wyld, Henry, 34

167

DATE DUE

DEC 11 1986			
DEC 0 6 2002			
JAN 0 8			
GAYLORD			PRINTED IN U.S.A.